# FIRST AID IN ENGLISH

# READER

*by*

ANGUS MACIVER

# BOOK B

**The information in this edition
is correct to February 1989.**

© *Angus Maciver, 1983.*

ISBN 0 7169 5501 6

ROBERT GIBSON & SONS (Glasgow) LIMITED
17 Fitzroy Place, Glasgow, G3 7SF.

# PREFACE

There is nothing like **Interest** to get children to read well, to read widely, and to understand what they read. **The stories in this book are specially selected to arouse, maintain, and satisfy the interest of the pupils.** This interest helps the pupils to overcome many difficulties in the mechanics of diction and to attain an adequate speed of recital.

**The Interesting Facts are presented in pictorial form for ease in comprehension at this particular stage.** They have a direct bearing on the stories and provide adequate material for expansion of vocabulary and general knowledge.

The Questions on the Stories (Do You Remember?) are **in sequence** and demand not only that the pupils read carefully but also that they remember the salient points. The answers (oral or written) can be used as **a direct aid to Composition.**

The Development Exercises (Can You Tell?) endeavour to expand on certain statements in the matter read, and the questions are designed to give the pupils an opportunity to **express their thoughts and knowledge, simply and accurately.**

**A.M.**

# ACKNOWLEDGMENTS

We value highly the permission to include copyright material and are happy to put on record our indebtedness for:

DUCK'S DITTY, by Kenneth Grahame, by permission of the author's Executors and Messrs. Methuen & Co. Ltd.

OWL LIGHT, by M.E. Sargent, from "Chatterbox", by permission of Messrs. Dean & Son Ltd.

A RHYME OF HARVEST, by Lucy Diamond, from "One Hundred Poems for Children", edited by Herbert Strang, by permission of The Clarendon Press, Oxford.

BEDTIME, by Eleanor Farjeon, by permission of Messrs. Pearn, Pollinger & Higham Ltd.

THE SHEPHERD and GOOD-BYE, from "The Enid Blyton Poetry Book", by permission of Messrs. Methuen & Co. Ltd.

A CLEVER TRICK, adapted from "The Tidal Wave", from Lafcadio Hearn's "Gleanings in Buddha Fields", by permission of Messrs. Jonathan Cape Ltd.

A HOT LAND . . . INDIA, adapted from "India, Land of Contrasts", from "Round the Globe", by permission of Messrs. Frederick Warne & Co., Ltd.

THE STORY OF A RIVER, adapted from "The River", by R. Clough, from the "Jolly Book for Children", by permission of Messrs. W. & R. Chambers Ltd.

and for

MY DOG, by Emily Lewis, whom we have been unable to trace.

# CONTENTS

# THE KING AND THE GOOSEHERD

LONG ago, in a land across the sea, there lived a good king, who loved books more than anything else in the world.

One morning he was out walking in the country, where he had gone on holiday for a few days. As the sun was very hot, he stopped and sat down to rest on a seat under a tree. He took a book out of his pocket and tried to read it but, as he was very tired, he soon fell asleep.

When the king awoke, it was past noon. He rose, picked up his cane, and started for home. He had walked a mile or more, when he suddenly remembered his book. He felt for it in his pockets, but could not find it. He had left it under the tree.

The king did not wish to walk back so far. Neither did he wish to lose the book. What should he do?

5

"Perhaps I can find someone who will go for It," said the king to himself, as he looked about him.

At the foot of a hill, not far away, he saw a boy tending a flock of geese. The birds were eating the short grass and wading in a shallow brook.

The king walked towards the boy and said to him, "My boy! Do you know the seat under the tree? It is about a mile from here and close to the road-side. I have left my book there. I will give you this gold coin if you will get it for me."

The eyes of the boy sparkled when he saw the piece of money. "I would like to go," he said, "but I cannot leave the geese. They would run away and soon be lost."

" The geese will be all right," replied the king. " I will take good care of them."

" Take my whip," said the boy. " I will go for your book. Be sure to keep watch on the big gander. He is the leader, and the whole flock will follow him wherever he goes."

The king took the whip, and the boy set off to get the book. When some distance away, the lad stopped and called back, " If you want to keep them together, just crack the whip ! "

The king sat on a stone and laughed at the thought of being a gooseherd. It was not long until the geese discovered that their master had gone. With a great cackling and hissing, the birds went running across the meadow.

The king ran after them, but he could not run fast enough. He tried to crack the whip, but failed. To make matters worse, the geese flew over a fence and began to eat the flowers and vegetables in a garden.

About half-an-hour later, the goose-boy came back with the book. When he saw that the geese had run away, he began to scold.

"I have found the book and now you have lost the geese. I knew this would happen. You must help me to drive them out of the garden."

Without saying a word, the good king handed back the whip.

"Stand there at the end of the fence," ordered the boy. "When I crack the whip, you must shout with all your might."

8

The king did as he was told. The boy went into the garden and after a great deal of shouting and cracking of the whip all the geese returned to the meadow.

" I hope you will forgive me if I have not been a good gooseherd," said the king. " Here are two gold pieces—one for bringing my book and one for all the trouble I have caused you. You see, I am the king, and I am not used to such work."

" The king ! " cried the boy in surprise. " I did not know. I am sorry if I made you angry. You are a kind man, and everyone says that you are a good king."

" Yes," replied the king with a smile. " I may be a good king, but I am a poor gooseherd."

*(Adapted)*

9

## DO YOU REMEMBER ?

1. What is the name of the story ?
2. Where did the story take place ?
3. Why did the king sit on the seat ?
4. What happened when he began to read the book ?
5. When did he awake ?
6. Some time later, what did he miss ?
7. Who was near-by ?
8. What did the king ask him to do ?
9. What reward did the king promise him ?
10. How did the boy keep the geese together ?
11. What happened when the boy went away ?
12. Where did the geese go ?
13. What did the boy say when he returned ?
14. How did they clear the geese out of the garden ?
15. What reward did the king give the gooseherd ?

## MORE THAN ONE

A **FLOCK** OF SHEEP

A **HERD** OF CATTLE

A **SWARM** OF BEES

A **FLOCK** OF BIRDS

A **LITTER** OF PUPPIES

A **BROOD** OF CHICKENS

A **SHOAL** OF FISH

A **SCHOOL** OF WHALES

A **PACK** OF WOLVES

A **TROOP** OF MONKEYS

## CAN YOU TELL ?

1. A gooseherd is a person who looks after geese.
   What is a (a) cowherd, (b) shepherd, (c) swineherd ?

2. When the king awoke it was past **noon.**
   What is (a) noon, (b) mid-night, (c) morning, (d) after-noon, (e) evening, (f) sun-rise, (g) sun-set, (h) dawn?

3. A number of geese together is called a **gaggle** or a **flock.**

   What name is given to a number of :—
   cows, sheep, birds, bees, fish, puppies, trees, people ?

4. The king promised to give a **gold** piece to the boy.
   (a) Of what metal are these coins made ?

        Penny, Five penny piece
   (b) How many half pennies can I get for
        (1) a five penny piece.
        (2) a fifty penny piece.
   (c) How many new pennies can I get for (1) £1.
        (2) 50 half pennies.

5. We say one **goose** but say two **geese.**
   (a) We say one **cow** but say two ............
   (b) We say one **fox** but say two ............
   (c) We say one **fly** but say two ............
   (d) We say one **wolf** but say two ............
   (e) We say one **mouse** but say two ............

6. The **gander** was the head of the flock.
   (a) Give feminine of :—gander, bull, ram, Billy-goat, tom-cat.
   (b) Give feminine of :—king, prince, boy, brother, uncle.

7. The geese **cackled** and **hissed.**

   What sounds do these creatures make ?
   dog, cat, sheep, pig, donkey, wolf, lion, horse, frog, cow.

8. The boy **found** the book but the king **lost** the geese.

   What are the opposites of these words in the story ?
   land, loved, morning, hot, stopped, asleep, remembered, short, fast, sorry.

### SOME THINGS TO DO

Draw or make a model of the King's crown.

Write about the jewels in the crown.

Draw the Queen on her throne.

# ANDROCLES AND THE LION

THERE once lived a slave whose name was Androcles. His Roman master was very cruel and often beat him with a big stick. At last the poor slave could stand it no longer and he made up his mind to run away.

" I will leave this dreadful place, and go away into the country," he said to himself. " There I will be free, and my cruel master will not be able to find me."

Androcles knew that he would need to be very careful. If the soldiers caught him trying to escape, they would put him in prison. The slave waited until it was dark, and then slipped quietly out of the house. He made his way very carefully out of the town without being seen by any of the soldiers.

When he reached the country, Androcles ran as fast as he could. On and on he went until he came to a large forest. The slave walked for many hours through the woods. His clothes were torn by the thorny branches of the trees, and he was very hungry.

Suddenly he saw a large cave in the side of a hill.

" What a good hiding place ! " he cried. " No one will find me here ! "

Androcles entered the cave and soon found a cosy spot to rest. He was so tired and weary, that in a few minutes he was fast asleep.

The runaway slave had not slept very long, when he was wakened by a loud roar. There, at the

mouth of the cave and coming towards him, was a huge lion. To his surprise, the beast did not spring at him, but limped slowly to his side. The animal held up one of its front paws and moaned sadly, as if it was in need of help.

Very bravely, Androcles took hold of the paw and looked at it. At once he saw the cause of all the trouble. A large sharp thorn had stuck in the animal's foot, and the creature was suffering great pain. As gently as he could, the slave pulled out the thorn.

When the thorn was out, the lion was very pleased. The animal wagged its tail, purred like a big cat, and licked the hands of the man who had been so kind.

For three years, Androcles and the lion shared the same home. Every day, the great beast went out hunting and brought him back food. At night, the runaway slave slept in a cosy bed at the back of the cave. The lion lay near the mouth of the cave, so that Androcles would come to no harm.

One day, Androcles was walking in the forest, when he was captured by some Roman soldiers, who were hunting wild animals. Alas, they told him that he would be put to death, and that he would be torn to pieces by a lion.

On the day that he was to die, many people went to the great circus to watch the terrible sight. The emperor was there, and he was seated on a high throne. When all was ready, Androcles was left alone in the middle of the circus.

17

Soon a loud roar was heard, as a huge hungry lion was let loose. The animal, with red angry eyes and wide-open jaws, bounded swiftly towards the lonely slave in the middle of the circus. Everyone expected it to spring upon the man and crush him with a mighty blow from its paw.

Suddenly, when only a few feet away from poor Androcles, it stopped and sniffed the air. The people were silent. They had never seen anything like this before. The lion went slowly forward, wagged its tail, and rubbed its head against him, just like a pet cat at home. Androcles knew at once that it was his old friend who had lived with him in the cave.

The people were amazed at the strange sight and the emperor sent for Androcles. When the slave told him the wonderful story, the king was so pleased that he set him free and gave him the lion as a present.

For many years Androcles kept the lion as a pet, and they were always together. Everyone knew their story, and smiled or waved as they passed. The lion followed his master everywhere he went, and at night the faithful animal slept outside his door.

*(Adapted)*

## DO YOU REMEMBER ?

1. What is the name of the story ?
2. Why did Androcles run away ?
3. When did he slip quietly out of the house ?
4. What tore his clothes ?
5. What good hiding place did he find ?
6. What wakened him in the cave ?
7. How did the lion show that it was hurt ?
8. What caused the pain ?
9. How did Androcles help the suffering animal ?
10. How did the lion show that it was pleased ?
11. How long did they live together ?
12. Why did the lion sleep at the mouth of the cave ?
13. How was Androcles captured ?
14. How was he to be punished ?
15: Tell the story of what happened at the circus.

---

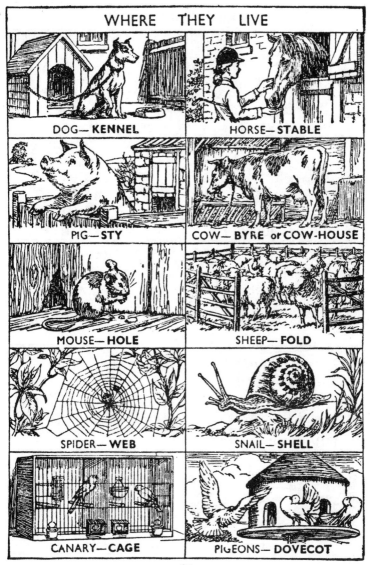

WHERE THEY LIVE

DOG—**KENNEL**

HORSE—**STABLE**

PIG—**STY**

COW—**BYRE** or **COW-HOUSE**

MOUSE—**HOLE**

SHEEP—**FOLD**

SPIDER—**WEB**

SNAIL—**SHELL**

CANARY—**CAGE**

PIGEONS—**DOVECOT**

WHERE THEY LIVE

LION— **CAVE or DEN**

BEAR— **DEN or CAVE**

RABBIT— **BURROW**

FOX— **EARTH**

BIRD— **NEST**

HARE— **FORM**

TAME RABBIT— **HUTCH**

HENS— **ROOST**

BEES— **HIVE**

WASPS— **NEST or BIKE**

## CAN YOU TELL ?

1. Where do these **tame** animals live ?
   (*a*) a horse, (*b*) a pig, (*c*) a dog, (*d*) a cow, (*e*) a sheep.

2. Where do these **wild** animals live ?
   (*a*) a lion, (*b*) a tiger, (*c*) a bear, (*d*) a fox, (*e*) a hare.

3. Name the homes of these **birds.**
   (*a*) a robin, (*b*) a canary, (*c*) a hen, (*d*) a parrot,
   (*e*) a cuckoo.

4. Where do these creatures stay ?
   (*a*) a bee, (*b*) a spider, (*c*) a snail, (*d*) a frog, (*e*) a wasp.

5. (*a*) A **tame** rabbit lives in a......................
   (*b*) A **wild** rabbit lives in a ......................
   (*c*) A **town** mouse lives in a ......................
   (*d*) A **field** mouse lives in a ......................
   (*e*) A **homing** pigeon lives in a ......................
   (*f*) A **wild** pigeon lives in a ......................

6. A lion has **fur.**
   Name creatures which have :—
   hair, fur, wool, feathers, scales.

7. The **lion** roars.
   Find the animal.
   (*a*) The ......... barks.  (*b*) The ......... purrs.
   (*c*) The ......... bleats.  (*d*) The ......... grunts.
   (*e*) The ......... squeaks.  (*f*) The ......... brays.
   (*g*) The ......... howls.  (*h*) The ......... lows.

8. Androcles kept the lion as a pet.

   Boys and girls keep all kinds of pets.

   Name any pets (*a*) which run about the house.
   (*b*) which are kept in cages.
   (*c*) which are kept in the garden.

---

## SOME THINGS TO DO

Draw a lion.

Imagine you are a lion tamer. Write about your work.

Draw or paint a scene from a circus.

# THE DUCK'S DITTY

ALL along the backwater,
   Through the rushes tall,
Ducks are a-dabbling,
Up, tails all.

Ducks' tails, drakes' tails,
Yellow feet a-quiver,
Yellow bills all out of sight,
Busy in the river.

Slushy green undergrowth,
Where the fishes swim,
Here we keep our larder,
Cool and full and dim.

Everyone for what he likes,
We like to be,
Heads down, tails up,
Dabbling free.

High in the blue above,
Swifts whirl and call,
We are down a-dabbling,
Up, tails all.

*Kenneth Grahame.*

# THE HEDGEHOG AND THE HARE

ONE bright summer morning, a little hedgehog was sitting at the door of his home. He was a merry little fellow who wished everybody to be happy.

" I think I'll just run over to the field and take a look at the turnips," he said to his wife.

" I hope you won't meet any of those rude hares," said Mrs. Hedgehog. " Yesterday, two of them came to the cabbage patch when our little ones and I were there. They laughed loudly at our short stumpy legs, and said that it must be terrible to be so slow."

" Do not worry about them," said her husband. " A hedgehog is as good as a hare any day. Cheerio ! I'll be back soon."

Just as Mr. Hedgehog reached the turnip field, he met a big bouncing hare on his way to the cabbage patch. This hare was proud, and thought himself a very fine fellow indeed because he could run like the wind.

When the little hedgehog saw the hare, he said in his best manner, " Good morning, Mr. Hare ! "

The hare did not answer this polite greeting, but said in a rude rough voice, " Why are *you* out so early this morning ? "

" I'm just taking a nice short walk for a breath of fresh air," replied the hedgehog.

27

"How can you enjoy a nice walk with such queer short legs?" said the hare. "By the way, I saw your wife and little ones yesterday. They were trying to run races, but not one of them could run faster than a tortoise. I nearly died laughing at them."

These rude remarks made the hedgehog very angry. "I suppose you think your long lanky legs are better than my short ones," he said. "If you are not afraid, I will run a race with you. I'll show you that I am much swifter than you."

"You! Swifter than I am!" said the hare with a laugh. "We must settle this matter at once. We'll race down the furrows between these

28

fine turnips. You run in one furrow, and I'll run in another. We shall soon see who will reach the other end first."

" I will not race with you just now," said the hedgehog. " I am very hungry and must go home for breakfast. I'll be back again in half-an-hour."

The hare said that he would wait for him, and the hedgehog went off home. " That rude hare is far too proud," said the little hedgehog to himself. " I'll teach him not to be so boastful."

When he reached home, he asked his wife to help him play a joke on the hare. " Here is my plan," he said. " You and I look so much alike that the hare cannot tell the difference between us. You must hide at the far end of the furrow. Just before the hare reaches you, pop up your head in front of him and say, ' I knew I could beat you quite easily '."

Soon they reached the field, and the little hedgehog placed his wife at the far end of the furrow. Then he went to the other end, where he found the hare waiting for him.

" Let us start at once," said the proud hare

" I am now quite ready," said the little hedgehog, as he took his place in his furrow.

The hare hopped into the next furrow and took his place. Then he called, " Ready, steady, go ! " and off he ran like the wind.

The little hedgehog ran only a few steps and then lay quite still among the leaves. Just before the hare reached the far end of the furrow, the hedgehog's wife popped up her head and said, " I knew I could beat you quite easily ! "

The hare stood still in wonder. " Well, I never ! " he exclaimed.

"Let that be a lesson to you," replied the hedgehog's wife.

"I will race you back," said the hare. "You cannot beat me again."

"Of course I can," answered Mrs. Hedgehog.

The hare turned quickly and ran back through his furrow even faster than before.

Just before he reached the other end, Mr. Hedgehog popped up his head and shouted, "Ha! Ha! I have beaten you again, Mr. Hare!"

"I cannot understand this at all," said the hare in amazement. "Let us try another race."

"Very well," replied Mr. Hedgehog.

31

This time the hare counted, " One, two, three ! " and was off like a shot from a gun. When he had almost reached the other end, Mrs. Hedgehog jumped up in front of him and said, " Well, Mr. Hare, I am first again ! "

" Race with me for the last time," begged the hare.

" All right," replied Mrs. Hedgehog.

Off the hare went down the furrow but again he was met by Mr. Hedgehog who said, " It is no use. I can beat you every time."

The hare was now too tired to run any more, and so he hopped slowly and sadly away.

The little hedgehogs laughed and laughed. " Brains are far better than legs," said Mr. Hedgehog to his happy little wife. " Mr. Hare will not be so proud next time we meet him."

*Grimm* (*Adapted*)

## DO YOU REMEMBER ?

1. What was the title of the story ?
2. Who was sitting at the door of his home ?
3. Which season of the year was it ?
4. What did Mrs. Hedgehog say about the hares ?
5. Who met Mr. Hedgehog at the turnip field ?
6. Where was Mr. Hare going ?
7. Why did the hedgehog become very angry ?
8. What did the hedgehog ask the hare to do ?
9. What did Mr. Hare say ?
10. Why did Mr. Hedgehog not run the race at once ?
11. What did the hedgehog ask his wife to do ?
12. How did they start the race ?
13. What happened the first time ? the second time ? the third time ? the fourth time ?
14. Why did the hare give up ?
15. What did Mr. Hedgehog say to his wife ?

33

# LIMBS

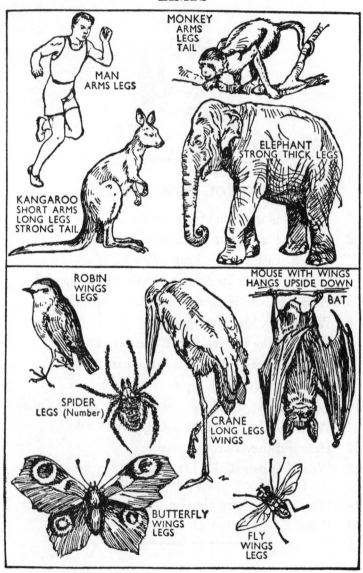

MONKEY
ARMS
LEGS
TAIL

MAN
ARMS LEGS

ELEPHANT
STRONG THICK LEGS

KANGAROO
SHORT ARMS
LONG LEGS
STRONG TAIL

ROBIN
WINGS
LEGS

MOUSE WITH WINGS
HANGS UPSIDE DOWN

BAT

SPIDER
LEGS (Number)

CRANE
LONG LEGS
WINGS

BUTTERFLY
WINGS
LEGS

FLY
WINGS
LEGS

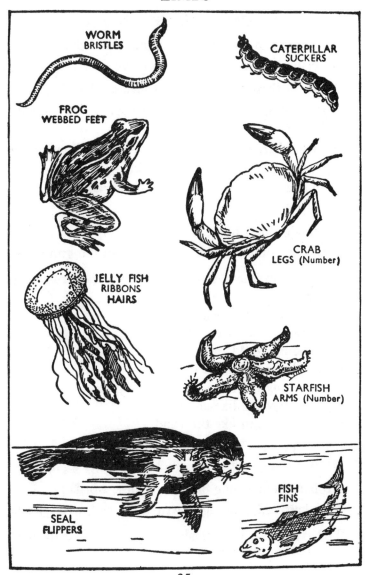

WORM
BRISTLES

CATERPILLAR
SUCKERS

FROG
WEBBED FEET

CRAB
LEGS (Number)

JELLY FISH
RIBBONS
HAIRS

STARFISH
ARMS (Number)

SEAL
FLIPPERS

FISH
FINS

## CAN YOU TELL ?

1. (*a*) Name two creatures which move swiftly.
   (*b*) Name two creatures which move slowly.

2. Which of these are good and which are bad ?
   rude, polite, rough, gentle, noisy, quiet, rowdy, mannerly.

3. We say " Mr. and **Mrs.**" Complete the following :—
   (1) father and............  (2) brother and ...............
   (3) boy and  ............  (4) husband and  ............
   (5) uncle and ............

4. The hedgehog's home is in a burrow.
   Name any other animals which live in the ground.

5. In which of these sentences did the boy run very quickly ?
   (1) The boy ran like a deer.
   (2) The boy ran like a snail.
   (3) The boy ran like lightning.
   (4) The boy ran like a tortoise.
   (5) The boy ran like a shot from a gun.
   (6) The boy ran like an elephant.
   (7) The boy ran like the wind.

6. (*a*) Name any creatures which have long legs.
   (*b*) Name any creatures which have short legs.

7. Explain the meaning of each of these words :—
   hare, hair, tail, tale, right, write, sale, sail, week, weak.

8. Tell as much as you can about a (1) hare, (2) hedgehog.

## OWL-LIGHT

WHEN the pale moon rises above the sea,
    The owl flies out of the ivy tree,
And the small birds quiver, the little mice quake,
As he goes his way by the wood and lake,
And his odd notes echo the farm-yard through—
That weird old cry—" Tu-whit-tu-whoo ! "

The light is dim in the fields and lanes,
As the children peep through the window-panes,
When the notes ring out in the silent night,
As the owl goes by with his noiseless flight,
And the cheeky sparrows go home to bed,
When " Tu-whit-tu-whoo " sounds overhead.

                                        *M. E. Sargent.*

# THE PRINCESS AND THE SHEPHERD

FAR across the sea, there once lived a very beautiful princess named Rose. The princess was the king's only daughter and he was very, very fond of her.

Princess Rose grew from a lovely child into a beautiful maiden. Many men came from far and near to seek to marry her. She refused all of them. Some wished to marry her for her riches, and the others wanted only to become king when her father died.

At last the king made up his mind to try out a clever plan. He told the princess in secret, and she at once agreed to it.

Here was the plan.

The princess was to dress in rags and wander

through her father's kingdom. She had not to tell anyone that she was really a princess. When she returned, she would wed the man who had shown her the greatest kindness.

The princess changed her rich gown and jewels for a tattered dress, a pair of old shoes, and a cheap shawl to cover her head. Early next morning, before anyone was awake, she slipped out of the palace without being seen.

The princess walked on and on for many miles, until at last she sat by the roadside to take a rest. While she was resting there, a proud young man came galloping along on his big white war-horse. She stepped out into the roadway and stopped him.

" Kind sir," said the princess. " I am tired
and have a long way to go. Could you please
take me part of the way ? "

" Indeed ! " cried the man. " I will do nothing
of the kind ! Out of my way ! " He struck the
horse with his spurs, and away he sped in a cloud
of dust.

" A very proud selfish man," said the princess
to herself.

On walked the princess, until she came to a
castle. As she was passing the gateway, she
met a man who was riding on a pony.

" What are you doing here ? " he shouted.

" I seek shelter and rest," said the princess.
" I have travelled far and I am very tired."

" Clear out of here at once ! " roared the angry
man.

At his cruel words, the princess turned and
hurried off down the road.

After a time, she met a rich merchant. He was
leading his donkeys, which were heavily laden
with all kinds of goods.

The princess stopped him and said, " I am
very tired and hungry. Could you spare me a
little food ? "

"You can starve for all I care," replied the man. "Be off with you!"

The poor sad princess turned away. No one had shown her any kindness since she had left the palace.

It so happened that a young shepherd saw the princess as she came along the dusty highway.

"Hullo!" he called to her. "You look very tired. Come over here and rest a-while."

She did so very thankfully. The princess sat down, took off her old shoes, and rubbed her sore feet.

" You must be hungry too," said the shepherd.
" You will share my lunch with me."

From a bag slung over his shoulder, he took
out a slice of bread, a piece of cake, a horn of
milk, and a mug.

The shepherd carefully wiped the mug and
filled it with milk. He offered it to the princess,
who thanked him and drank it thirstily. Then he
offered her the cake, but she made him break it
in half, so that they both had a piece. They
laughed and talked about different things. At
last the princess said that she must go on her way.

The princess was now very happy, because she had found someone who was good and kind. She returned to the palace, and went at once to see her father.

" Well, daughter ! " said the king. " Did you meet anyone who was worthy to be your husband ? "

" Yes, father ! " replied the princess. " The only one who showed me any kindness was a shepherd. He even shared his food with me, when I was hungry and thirsty."

" A shepherd ! Well ! Well ! " said the king in surprise. " Let him be brought to the palace till we see him."

The shepherd, whose name was David, was summoned to the palace. He did not know why he should be asked to attend the royal court, and he was a little afraid.

The shepherd entered the great throne-room. When he saw the king and the queen, he bowed low before them.

" Are you the young shepherd who shared his lunch with a poor beggar-maid ? " asked the king.

" Yes ! " replied David. " She was tired and hungry and I could not let her starve."

Suddenly the princess appeared, and the shepherd stared at her in surprise. He knew then that the poor girl he had helped was none other than Princess Rose.

The king smiled, so did the queen, and everyone gleefully clapped their hands. The young couple were married soon afterwards, and they lived very happily together.

## DO YOU REMEMBER?

1. What is the title of the story?
2. How many children had the king?
3. What was the name of the princess?
4. How did she change to a beggar-maid?
5. What did she say to the man on the white horse?
6. What was his reply?
7. What did she say to the horseman at the castle?
8. What was his reply?
9. What did she say to the rich merchant?
10. What was his reply?
11. Who was the first to show any kindness to the princess?
12. What did she share with him?
13. What order was sent to the shepherd?
14. Why did he stare at the princess in surprise?
15. How did the story end?

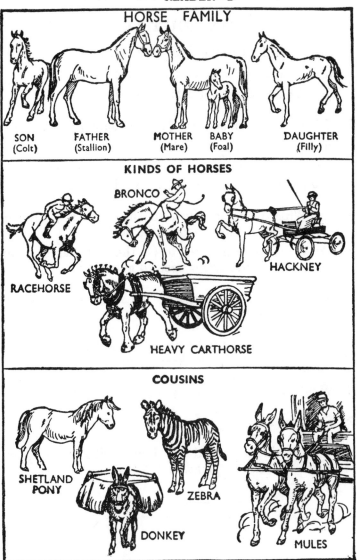

# HORSE FAMILY

SON (Colt)    FATHER (Stallion)    MOTHER (Mare)    BABY (Foal)    DAUGHTER (Filly)

## KINDS OF HORSES

BRONCO

HACKNEY

RACEHORSE

HEAVY CARTHORSE

## COUSINS

SHETLAND PONY

ZEBRA

DONKEY

MULES

## CAN YOU TELL ?

1. (*a*) What does a king wear on his head ?
   (*b*) What name is given to a king's home ?
   (*c*) What is the royal chair called ?

2. Fill in the blank spaces. No. 1 is done for you.
   prince...princess, shepherd............., giant.............,
   king........., man........., lion........., waiter.........,
   gentleman........., son........., conductor.........

3. (*a*) What name is given to the horse's (1) home,
   (2) feet, (3) long hair on its neck ?
   (*b*) What name is given to (1) the seat placed on its
   back, (2) the straps used to guide it ?

4. What is a (1) shepherd, (2) dentist, (3) artist,
   (4) merchant, (5) pedlar ?

5. Describe a (1) war-horse, (2) race-horse, (3) carthorse, (4) pony, (5) donkey, (6) mule.

6. What sound is made by a (1) horse, (2) donkey ?

7. Describe a castle.

8. The shepherd shared his lunch with the beggar-
   maid. Describe a picnic lunch.

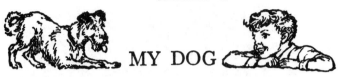 MY DOG

HAVE you seen a little dog anywhere about ?
  A raggy dog, a shaggy dog, who's always
    looking out
For some fresh mischief which he thinks he really
  ought to do.
He's very likely, at this minute, biting someone's
  shoe.

If you see that little dog, his tail up in the air,
A whirly tail, a curly tail, a dog who doesn't care
For any other dog he meets, not even for himself;
Then hide your mats, and put your meat upon the
  topmost shelf.

If you see a little dog, barking at the cars,
A raggy dog, a shaggy dog, with eyes like twinkling
  stars,
Just let me know, for though he's bad, as bad as
  bad can be;
I wouldn't change that dog for all the treasures of
  the sea.

*Emily Lewis.*

49

# A STRANGE TREASURE

OLD John Crabtree was the owner of the biggest orchard in his part of the country. He was also the father of three strong, but lazy, sons.

Old John looked after his fruit trees with very little help from his sons. Early every morning, while they were still in bed, the old man could be found working alone in the orchard. He dug the soil, cut away all the useless branches from the old trees, carefully tended the young trees, and picked all the fruit at harvest time.

Every evening after his work, he would sit on a log and rest in the shade of his trees. Old John would gaze and gaze at the long rows of apple trees, pear trees, and plum trees. Then he would sigh to think that soon he would be too old to give them all the care they needed.

"Dear me!" he would say to himself. "It is a great pity. I wish my sons would work in the orchard. If they did, I am sure that the fruit would bring them a fortune."

There came a time when John no longer worked among his fruit trees, for he took ill and died.

Not long after his death, the three sons met to hear what money their father had left to them. The reading of his will amazed them, because there was only this one sentence:—

"The orchard, and the treasure which is there, I leave to my three sons."

The sons stared at each other in astonishment. " Treasure ! " they shouted. " Isn't that wonderful ? We will be rich ! Father has hidden his money in the orchard ! "

" We must be very careful," said the eldest son. " If we tell others of this, they might steal the treasure from us."

" What shall we do ? " asked the youngest son.

" We must tell no one about the treasure," said the middle son. " We will dig and search in the orchard until we find it."

The sons then made their plans to find the treasure. They divided the orchard into three parts, and worked as they had never worked before.

They carefully dug the soil from one end of the orchard to the other. They even turned over the earth around the roots. Not an inch did they miss. Alas ! After days, and weeks, and months of digging and searching, no treasure was found.

That year, however, something happened which had never happened before. There was so much fruit on the trees, that the branches were bent almost to the ground. The three sons were delighted. Never had they seen such a crop of apples and pears and plums.

When harvest time came, the sons were kept

53

very busy. The youngest son picked the ripe fruit from the trees, the middle son cleaned it, and the eldest son packed it carefully into boxes. The fruit was then sold to merchants for a very good price.

So much money did they get, they became quite rich.

One day the eldest son said to his brothers, " I wonder what our father meant, when he said there was a treasure in the orchard ? "

" Our father was a very wise and truthful man," replied the youngest brother. " There must

54

be treasure there, only we cannot find it."

" Do you know what I think ? " said the middle brother. " Father knew that we were very lazy, and would not take care of the fruit trees. If he said there was treasure in the orchard, he knew that we would dig and search for it. By our digging, we helped the trees to give us such a wonderful crop of fruit."

" Yes," replied the eldest brother. " I think that you are right. Father was very clever. The fruit has brought us a great deal of money and made us rich."

Each year, the three sons worked hard in the orchard. They found no money hidden in a box below the ground, but each year the orchard gave them another kind of treasure.

*Aesop (Adapted)*

———

## DO YOU REMEMBER ?

1. What was the title of the story ?
2. What was the father's name ?
3. What did he own ?
4. How many sons had he ?
5. What kind of sons were they ?
6. How did Old John look after his orchard ?
7. What happened to him ?
8. What did he say in his will ?
9. Why were his sons so joyful ?
10. What did they do ?
11. What treasure did they find ?
12. What happened for the first time that year ?
13. How did the sons gather the fruit ?
14. How did they become rich ?
15. What treasure did the sons get from the orchard ?

---

# FRUITS FROM TREES

APPLE

PEAR

PLUM

CHERRY

ORANGE

GRAPE

BANANA

COCONUT

## CAN YOU TELL ?

1. Which of these are **fruits** :—

   carrot, orange, daisy, banana, rose, cabbage, violet, cherry, buttercup, potato, turnip, tulip, grape, onion, lemon ?

2. You would buy apples, plums and pears at a **fruit-shop.**
   Where would you buy :—meat, milk, cakes, fish, sugar ?

3. What **colour** is a ripe (*a*) banana, (*b*) apple, (*c*) plum, (*d*) strawberry, (*e*) pear, (*f*) gooseberry ?

4.
   | *One* | *More than one* |
   |-------|-----------------|
   | leaf | ............... |
   | man | ............... |
   | foot | ............... |
   | daisy | ............... |
   | tooth | ............... |

5. We say " an orchard of **fruit trees.**"
   string, coal, matches, jam, milk.
   Put these words in their right places.
   a jug of............, a bag of............, a pot of............,
   a box of............, a ball of............

6. Old John was **not lazy.**
   Give one word instead of the two words underlined.
   (*a*) The spelling was **not easy,** (*b*) The door was **not open.** (*c*) The sum was **not right.** (*d*) The paper was **not clean.** (*e*) The coat was **not wet.**

## THE CRICKET MATCH

WALKING along Olympic Way one day Anansi, the spider, saw that a Cricket match was in progress. He was strolling through the gate when the gate-man asked him for a dollar. "I have no money." said Anansi.

"No money!" said the man. "Do you not know that spiders are only allowed in free on Sundays? Today is Friday and you cannot get in."

As Anansi sat sadly on Seaward School wall he saw a man fanning himself with his hat. "Ah, ha!" thought Anansi, "If I got into his hat no one would see me. With a leap he was inside the hat. When the man reached the pay gate he put on his hat, paid his dollar and went into the cricket ground. The man felt warm again and as he took off his hat Anansi jumped to the ground.

With all this effort Anansi felt hot and thirsty. Looking round he saw a little girl with an ice lolly. When she wasn't looking Anansi stood on top of the lollipop and waved three or four of his legs. When the little girl saw him she screamed and threw away the lolly. Anansi enjoyed it very much and ate until he fell asleep under a bush.

When Anansi wakened he saw his friend Rat looking at the lollipop. Anansi asked him if he would like to have a bite. When Rat nodded his head Anansi said he could try the lolly at 10 cents a bite. Rat said that was too much as most of the lolly had melted. They finally agreed on two cents a lick and Rat with nine licks finished the lot. He also ate the stick, for which Anansi charged two cents extra.

By this time the cricket match was finished and, sad to say, Anansi had seen none of it.

# 10

## A KIND-HEARTED BOY

ONCE there was a kind-hearted boy named Abraham Lincoln. For short, his friends called him Abe. He lived with his father, mother, and sister in a log cabin on a little farm. They were very poor and his father had a hard time to make a living.

One day his father said to the family, " I have sold the farm. This land is too poor to grow good crops. Tomorrow we will move to another place where the soil is better for farming."

Now in those days there were no railways and people had to travel from one place to another on horseback or in waggons. The family put all their belongings into a large covered waggon and, with two strong oxen to pull it, they set off to find a new home.

61

It was almost the end of winter and the roads were deep in slush and mud. Quite often the waggon wheels sank down in the road and they had a hard task to pull them out. Sometimes they had to take their furniture out of the waggon before they could manage to move the wheels.

Mr. Lincoln led the faithful animals and kept them on the right way but now and again he could not avoid trouble. The journey was very slow and tiresome but they struggled on as best they could.

In that part of the country there were no bridges over the streams which they had to cross. It was a very long, cold, and lonely trail. At night they stopped beside a stream and made a fire. After supper all slept in the waggon which gave them shelter from the cold wind.

During the day Abe walked beside the oxen and sometimes he patted them on the back as they pulled their heavy load. His mother and sister sat in the waggon although the road was often rough and bumpy.

There was another traveller—one that has not been spoken about so far—Abe's pet puppy dog. The little animal seemed to enjoy every moment of the journey. To him, it was great fun to chase the rabbits and to send the squirrels scurrying up the trees.

One day the young dog chased a rabbit far into the woods. While he was away, the oxen had pulled the waggon, with the whole family inside, through a wide frozen stream. The thin ice had broken under the heavy weight but the brave animals had trudged through the icy water.

The family had gone on some distance when they heard a loud barking behind them. Mr. Lincoln stopped the waggon to find out the cause of all the noise. When they looked back they saw that the little dog had been left behind on the other side of the stream. He was running up and down the bank and barking with all his might.

Abe ran back and tried to coax him to cross. The frightened little creature refused as he was afraid that he would fall through the thin ice.

"We shall have to go on without him as we cannot turn back," said Mr. Lincoln.

"We cannot be so cruel as to leave him," replied Abe. "My poor little dog will starve or freeze to death."

Before his father could say any more, Abe sat down and quickly pulled off his boots and stockings. He then waded through the cold water which, at times, reached to his knees. When he arrived at the other side, the happy little dog jumped all over him in his joy.

Abe took the timid creature in his arms and waded back across the stream. While he was putting on his boots and stockings, the puppy licked his hands and face to show his thanks.

For the rest of the journey the young dog kept close to the boy's side. When the puppy saw any rabbits or squirrels he would give a loud " Bow-wow ! " but he would not run after them. He had found out that a good friend was worth more than all the rabbits and squirrels in the world.

This kind-hearted boy became one of the greatest presidents of the United States of America. It can truly be said that people who are really great are always kind.

(*Adapted*)

66

# A KIND-HEARTED BOY

## DO YOU REMEMBER ?

1. What is the name of the story ?
2. Who was the kind-hearted boy ?
3. With whom did he live ?
4. Where did he live ?
5. Why did his father sell the farm ?
6. How did people travel in those days ?
7. When did they set off to find a new home ?
8. Why was it a slow and tiresome journey ?
9. Where did they stop to rest at night ?
10. What pet had Abe brought with him ?
11. How did the little animal enjoy himself ?
12. How was the puppy left behind ?
13. Why did the little dog refuse to cross the stream ?
14. What did Abe do ?
15. What did this kind-hearted boy become ?

# MEANS OF TRAVEL

# MEANS OF TRAVEL

REINDEER

HUSKIES

SKIS

RICKSHAW—SINGAPORE

CAMEL

AMERICAN SHEPHERD

CABLECAR—SINGAPORE

## CAN YOU TELL?

1. The little dog gave a loud " Bow-wow ! "
   Which creatures make these sounds ?
   " Moo ! " " Me-ow ! " " Baa ! " " Cock-a-doodle-do ! " " Hee-haw ! "

2. **Abraham** was called **Abe** for short.
   What are the short names for :—Samuel, Frederick, Thomas, William, Joseph ?

3. A **puppy** is a **young dog.**
   What is a :—kitten, lamb, calf, piglet, chicken ?

4. (*a*) A **farmer** is a person who farms.
   What is a :—dancer, singer, driver, skater, painter ?
   (*b*) A **visitor** is a person who visits.
   What is a :—sailor, instructor, doctor, conductor, tailor ?

5. A **stream** is made of **water.**
   Which of these are made of water ?
   river, forest, street, sea, lake, mountain, pond, cliff, island, ice.

6. Young Abe lived in a **log cabin.**
   Who lives in a :—palace, wigwam, igloo, prison, barracks ?

7. Abe **waded** across the stream.
   Explain how you do these in water :—wading, diving, swimming, paddling, floating.

8. Two strong **oxen** pulled the waggon.
   What other animals are used to pull or carry loads ?

---

# 11

## BEDTIME

FIVE minutes, five minutes more, please !
Let me stay five minutes more
Can't I just finish the castle
I'm building here on the floor ?
Can't I just finish the story
I'm reading here in my book ?
Can't I just finish this bead-chain
It is almost finished—look !
Can't I just finish this game, please ?
When a game is once begun
It's a pity never to find out
Whether you've lost or won.
Can't I just stay *five* minutes ?
Well, can't I stay just *four* ?
*Three* minutes, then ? *Two* minutes ?
Can't I stay *one* minute more ?

*Eleanor Farjeon.*

71

## A CLEVER TRICK

ONCE upon a time, there lived in far-away Japan, a very good and wise old farmer named Tama. His little grandson, who was called Yone, stayed with him. All around the house, which stood on a high hill, lay big rice-fields.

The people, who worked on the farm, lived in houses at the foot of the hill and near the sea-shore. Every morning, they climbed up the hill to work in the fields. Every evening they returned to their homes down in the village.

Everybody was happy. It was autumn, and the rice had grown ripe and was ready for cutting. The crop would be heavy, and there would be plenty to eat.

One day, when his workers had all gone down to their homes near the shore, old Tama and little

Yone stood on the top of the hill. They watched the sun set over the sea. Far away in the distance, where the sea seemed to meet the sky, the old man saw a strange sight which puzzled him at first.

It was a great tall black cloud, stretching from the water high into the sky. It was moving quickly over the sea towards them.

" Quick ! " cried old Tama to little Yone. " Run to the house, and bring me two lighted sticks from the fire ! "

Poor little Yone wondered what was wrong, because his grandfather had often warned him against touching the fire. However, the boy ran as hard as he could, and soon returned with the burning sticks.

Old Tama grabbed hold of one of the torches and began to set fire to the rice-field. Yone could hardly believe his eyes, and he thought that his grandfather had suddenly gone mad.

"Hurry!" cried the old man. "Help me to put the field on fire!"

Yone burst into tears, but he did as he was told. The rice quickly caught fire, and the field was soon ablaze.

Suddenly a loud shout was heard from the village below, and many people came running up the hill. They reached the field and tried to stamp out the fire with their feet. Some of the men ran quickly to the worst places, and beat upon the flames with

sticks. Even the women came to help and they had brought their children with them. Soon there was not a single person in the village.

When they had put out the fire, some of the men turned to old Tama.

" See what you have done ! " they shouted. " You have spoiled this good field of rice ! Why did you do it ? You must be mad ! "

The old man smiled, and waved his arm towards the sea.

" Look ! " he cried. " You were all in great danger "

The people looked, and saw the great tall black cloud in the sky. In the sea below, they saw a giant wave coming swiftly towards the shore. Every one stood in silence, as a great wall of water struck their village with a noise like thunder. They watched the sea batter down their little houses, and sweep them all away.

The people again turned to old Tama, but this time they were shouting with joy. They now knew why he had set the rice-field on fire. It was the only way by which he could make everybody leave the village quickly. When they had rushed up the hill to put out the fire, they had run away from danger.

The people did not care that the rice-field was burnt, nor that they had lost their homes. They knew that wise old Tama, by his clever trick, had saved their lives.

(*Adapted*)

## DO YOU REMEMBER ?

1. What is the name of the story ?
2. Where did the story take place ?
3. What was the old farmer called ?
4. Where was his farm ?
5. Where did his workers stay ?
6. What was the name of the little boy ?
7. What time of year was it ?
8. What strange sight did Tama see ?
9. What did he ask Yone to fetch him ?
10. What did the old man do with the burning stick
11. Who came to put out the fire ?
12. What did they say to Tama ?
13. What answer did the old farmer give ?
14. What did they see from the hill ?
15. Why did the people shout with joy ?

---

RICE

PLANTING

PLOUGHING

GATHERING THE HARVEST

RICE PLANT

SEPARATING THE GRAIN FROM THE STALK

## CAN YOU TELL ?

1. A **farmer** is a person who **farms**.

   What is a baker, cleaner, teacher, explorer, slater ?
   Here are some harder ones.
   What is a cobbler, butcher, barber, plumber, porter ?

2. It was **autumn** and the crop was ready for cutting.

   Which season is it ?
   (*a*) When the birds are making their nests.
   (*b*) When we go to the seaside and play in the sun.
   (*c*) When the leaves are falling from the trees.
   (*d*) When the snow is lying on the ground.

3. (*a*) Why does a farmer keep (1) cows, (2) hens,
   (3) sheep, (4) pigs ?

   (*b*) What kinds of crops are grown on a farm ?

4. The **rice** was growing in a **field**.

   What grows in a (1) forest, (2) garden, (3) field,
   (4) meadow, (5) orchard ?

5. The **fire** was put out **with sticks and feet**.

   How is a fire put out in a (*a*) forest, (*b*) house in the
   country, (*c*) house in the town, (*d*) hedge, (*e*) ship ?

6. The sun **rises** in the east and **sets** in the west.

   (*a*) Which side of the school is sunny in the morning ?
   (*b*) Which side of the school is sunny in the after-
   noon ?
   (*c*) Point to East, West, North, South.

# THE MOON

THE moon has a face like the clock in the hall;
    She shines on thieves on the garden wall,
On streets and fields and harbour quays,
And birdies asleep on the forks of the trees.

The squalling cat and the squeaking mouse,
The howling dog by the door of the house,
The bat that lies in bed at noon,
All love to be out by the light of the moon.

But all of the things that belong to the day,
Cuddle to sleep to be out of the way;
And flowers and children close their eyes,
Till up in the morning the sun shall arise.

*R. L. Stevenson.*

## THE GOLDEN TOUCH

IN a far-away land, there once lived a king whose name was Midas. Although Midas was very rich, he was not happy, because he wanted more gold and more gold and more gold.

One morning as he sat counting his money, a bright sunbeam came darting in through the window. The king stopped in surprise. There, perched on the sunbeam, was the gayest little fairy

you ever saw. She had golden hair, a golden dress, and golden shoes.

When the fairy saw that the king was sad, she asked, " Midas ! Why are you so unhappy ? What is it that you wish ? "

Midas said, " I have been saving my gold for years and years, and yet I cannot get enough. I sometimes wish that everything I touch would turn to gold."

" Are you sure you would like that ? " asked the fairy.

" Of course ! " said Midas. " I would then be the richest and happiest man in the world."

" All right," replied the fairy. " At day-break to-morrow you shall have your wish."

Next morning King Midas rose at dawn. As soon as he touched his clothes, they turned into beautiful golden robes. He walked proudly from his room. On his way down the stairs, he touched the shining wooden railing. At once it became bright gold. Oh, how happy he was!

Midas went into the garden. He touched the flowers, and all turned to bright shining gold. Then he returned and entered his dining-hall. There he saw the table laid for breakfast. As the king wished to please his little daughter Marigold, he touched the small blue bowl from which she always drank her milk. It too turned to gold.

Suddenly Marigold came running in from the

garden. She was crying, and in her hand she held a stiff golden rose.

" Look ! " she cried. " All the flowers have become stiff and hard and ugly. A cruel fairy must have done it."

When she sat down to breakfast she looked for her bowl. " This is dreadful ! " she said. " Even my nice little blue bowl has changed."

The king was very sad to see his little daughter so unhappy. Kindly he said to her, " Do not worry, Marigold. The flowers and the bowl are now worth more than ever. You will soon learn to love them."

Midas did not know that the golden touch was to bring him great sorrow. As soon as he tried to eat, he found that every bit of food he touched was turned to gold. Although the table was covered with the best of food, poor King Midas could not eat anything.

When Marigold finished her breakfast, she ran to her father. Very tenderly, he touched her hair. To his horror, his little girl turned to gold. His gentle Marigold, whom he loved so dearly, would never be able to speak to him again. How unhappy he was! Now he knew that gold was not the greatest thing in the world.

Just then a golden sunbeam entered the room.

On the sunbeam stood the same gay fairy.

" Why are you so sad ? " she asked. " Are you not pleased with your wish ? "

" No ! " cried Midas. " Take away the golden touch ! See what it has done to my lovely Marigold ! Please give my little girl back to me ! "

" I am very glad that you have learned a lesson. There are many things better than gold. If you wish to rid yourself of the golden touch, bathe yourself in the river. Afterwards, pour a little water from the river on everything you have turned to gold."

King Midas hurried to the river and bathed himself. He also carried a large jug of water from the river to the palace. Soon he had his darling Marigold again. How happy they were !

Together they went into the garden and changed the hard golden flowers to lovely soft sweet-smelling blossoms.

" What a dreadful place this world would be, if everything was made of gold ! " said King Midas.

" Yes ! " replied Marigold. " Everything which is soft and warm and beautiful would become hard and cold and ugly."

*(Adapted)*

## DO YOU REMEMBER ?

1. What is the name of the story ?
2. Who was king of this far-away land ?
3. Why was he very unhappy ?
4. How did the little fairy enter the room ?
5. How was she dressed ?
6. What wish did King Midas make ?
7. When was his wish granted ?
8. What did the king first turn to gold ?
9. What did he next turn to gold ?
10. What did Midas do in the garden ?
11. How did he try to please his little daughter ?
12. What did Marigold say about the changes ?
13. Why was the king unable to eat ?
14. What happened when he touched his daughter's hair ?
15. How did the king rid himself of the golden touch ?

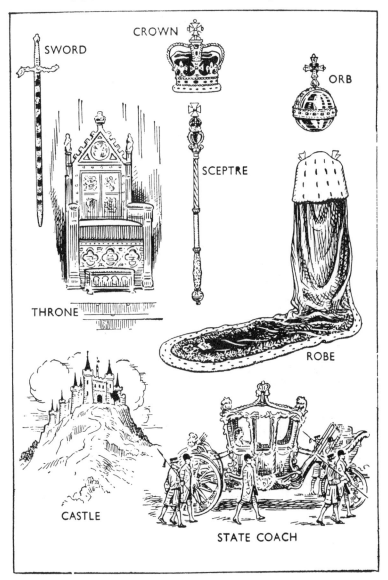

SWORD

CROWN

ORB

SCEPTRE

THRONE

ROBE

CASTLE

STATE COACH

## CAN YOU TELL ?

1. They were in the story you have just read.
   Who was (*a*) greedy and selfish, (*b*) lovely and gentle,
   (*c*) tiny and gay ?

2. Midas was a **king.**
   What is the title given to a king's (*a*) wife, (*b*) daughter,
   (*c*) son ?

3. King Midas had a **garden.**
   (*a*) What is a garden ?
   (*b*) Name some garden flowers.

4. The story tells of a **fairy.**
   Name other kinds of little magic folk.

5. You use your **hands** to **touch.**
   What do you use to (*a*) hear, (*b*) see, (*c*) smell,
   (*d*) taste ?

6. **Marigold** is the name of a **flower.**
   What other flowers are often used as names for girls ?

7. **Gold** is a **metal** which is dug out of the ground.
   Name some other metals.

8. Describe what is on a table which is laid for (*a*)
   breakfast, (*b*) dinner, (*c*) supper.

---

# BRER RABBIT GOES FISHING

BRER RABBIT and Brer Fox were just like some boys and girls. They were always playing jokes and tricks on each other.

One day in summer, Brer Rabbit, Brer Fox, and Brer Bear were digging a patch of ground so that they could plant some corn. The sun was very hot and Brer Rabbit soon felt tired. He did not tell the others because he was afraid that they would say he was lazy.

91

Suddenly Brer Rabbit had an idea. He carried off a bundle of grass, and piled it on a rubbish heap which was some distance away. While the others were still digging, he took the chance to slip away and try to find a cool resting-place.

A few minutes later he spied a well with a bucket hanging in it.

" That bucket looks fine and cool," said Brer Rabbit to himself. " I'll jump into it and take a nice short nap."

He jumped from the wall of the well into the bucket. At once the bucket went down the well at great speed. Brer Rabbit was frightened. He did not know where he was going.

Suddenly he felt the bucket hit the water with a loud splash. Brer Rabbit was almost drowned but, lucky for him, the bucket kept afloat.

Another thing had frightened him. While he was coming down he had seen another bucket fly past him on its way to the top of the well.

Poor Brer Rabbit ! He just lay in the bucket and shook and shivered.

Now Brer Fox, who always kept an eye on Brer Rabbit, had watched him sneak away from the rubbish heap. He thought that Brer Rabbit was up to another of his pranks so he made up his mind to follow him. Brer Fox saw Brer Rabbit

93

jump into the bucket and disappear down the well.

" My goodness ! " said Brer Fox in surprise. " Where has he gone ? It must be a secret hiding-place. I wonder if he keeps his money down there Perhaps it is a gold-mine and Brer Rabbit does not want anyone to know about it. I've caught him this time. I will find out why he has gone down the well."

Brer Fox crept up to the well and listened, but he could hear no sound. He jumped to the top of the wall and peeped down. He could see nothing as it was very dark at the bottom.

" Hullo, Brer Rabbit ! What are you doing down there ? " he called.

Brer Rabbit, who was afraid to move in case he would upset the bucket, shouted back, " What am I doing ? I'm fishing, of course. I wanted to catch some fish for dinner and so give you all a great surprise."

" Have you caught any ? " asked Brer Fox.

" Yes. I have caught so many fish that my bucket is already full. I will need your help to carry them home."

" What kind of fish have you caught ? " said Brer Fox in wonder.

" All kinds. This place is full of them. I've kept only the big ones. I threw the little ones back into the water."

" How can I get down, Brer Rabbit ? "

" Quite easily," replied the other. " Jump into the bucket beside you and it will take you down safely."

Brer Rabbit talked on happily about his wonderful catch. Brer Fox soon became very jealous and jumped into the bucket. As he went down the well, the rope pulled up the other bucket containing Brer Rabbit. They passed each other half-way and Brer Rabbit sang out:

" Goodbye, Brer Fox, take care of your clothes,
For this is the way the old world goes,
Some go up and some go down !
You'll get to the bottom safe and sound."

At the top of the well Brer Rabbit hopped out and called, " Cheerio ! Now you will need to wait until some silly creature comes along to take your place."

Poor Brer Fox saw that he had been cleverly tricked. He was very sad as he sat in the bucket at the bottom of the well. There seemed to be no hope of rescue.

But Brer Rabbit did not mean to leave Brer Fox down the well for ever. He wanted more fun. He told the farmer that Brer Fox was splashing about in the well, and that the water was all muddy.

Half-an-hour later Brer Fox heard a loud noise at the top of the well. It was the farmer who had come to shoot him. Brer Fox made no sound and kept perfectly still.

Suddenly there was a jerk and Brer Fox felt himself being slowly pulled upwards. When he reached the top he gave one great leap from the bucket and ran off as fast as he could. The farmer shot at him but missed.

When Brer Fox reached the safety of the woods he lay down to rest.

" I must be more careful after this," he said to himself. " Brer Rabbit nearly caught me that time. I was very lucky to escape."

*(Adapted)*

## DO YOU REMEMBER ?

1. What is the name of the story ?
2. What were Brer Rabbit, Brer Fox, and Brer Bear doing ?
3. What kind of day was it ?
4. How did Brer Rabbit get away from the others ?
5. Where did he try to sleep ?
6. What happened when he jumped into the bucket ?
7. Who watched Brer Rabbit disappear down the well ?
8. Where did Brer Fox think he had gone ?
9. What did Brer Fox shout down the well ?
10. What was Brer Rabbit's answer ?
11. What did Brer Fox do ?
12. What did Brer Rabbit say as they passed each other ?
13. Why was Brer Fox very sad ?
14. Why did the farmer come to the well ?
15. How did Brer Fox escape ?

# STRANGE FISH

FLOUNDER

SHARK

SAWFISH

SWORDFISH

EEL

FLYING FISH

SEA HORSE

LUNG FISH

## CAN YOU TELL ?

1. Brer Rabbit **was digging** with **a spade.**
   Find the missing words :—
   (a) Mother cut the loaf of bread with a ..............
   (b) The barber cut his hair with a pair of ..............
   (c) The teacher wrote on the board with **a** piece of ...............
   (d) The joiner struck the nail with a ..............
   (e) The grocer weighed the cheese on his ..............

2. These **fish** are of **different sizes.** Place them in order (smallest first) :—herring, shark, goldfish, cod, minnow.

3. A **bucket** is used to **hold water.**

   Which of these are used to hold water :—bag, kettle, basket, bath, basin, box, tumbler, envelope, cupboard, boiler ?

4. Name different kinds of fish which are sold in fish shops.

5. The farmer got his **water** from the **well.**
   (a) How do you get water at home ?
   (b) From where does it come ?

6. It was **summer** and the sun **was very hot.**
   (a) Name the four seasons.
   (b) Which season do you like best ? Tell why.
   (c) Which time of day do you like best ? Tell why.

# 16

# THE STORY OF A RIVER

A TINY little spring burst out of the ground. "Plop, plop, plop," it said. As it ran down the hill-side, it whispered "Pitter, patter, pitter, patter." It had become a little stream.

The stream passed through a field and a little girl jumped over it. "Ha, ha!" laughed the stream. "You can jump over me now, but I am growing bigger and bigger." On it went, and soon it was joined by another stream, and another, and another. These other streams are called tributaries. Soon the little stream became quite big.

The stream came to a bridge. It was only a long plank of wood laid across, but the stream felt very proud. "I am too big to be jumped over now!" it cried. It danced on and on, until it reached some children.

" We can fish here ! " shouted one little boy.

" Fancy ! " said the stream. " I must be a river now. I am quite big, and children can fish and even bathe in me."

The river began to run more slowly. The land was flat, and fields of corn stood on each side. The river became stronger and stronger, and tore off bits of rock and soil where the bank was not wide enough. It swept the mud and sand

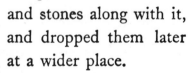

and stones along with it, and dropped them later at a wider place.

Suddenly the river ran into a village. What a proud moment that was !

" A real bridge of stone ! " cried the river. " Now I am so big that people must build a bridge to cross me ! "

After leaving the village it passed through many more fields, where cattle and sheep grazed on its banks.

A bigger surprise awaited it when it entered a small town. Here the river found itself carrying hundreds of little boats, all full of happy, cheerful people.

" The people here are very fond of me ! " It cried. " I wish I could stay here always, but I can't. I must go on. I don't know why, but I must go on."

On went the river, past more trees and green fields, until it came to a huge town called a city. At first it was pleased to see so many big bridges, but later it became very sad. Big pipes with dirty water ran into it, and many buildings with tall smoking chimneys stood on its banks.

"I don't like this place," moaned the river. "I am becoming very dirty, and people pay no attention to me."

The river flowed on and became wider and wider. Many large boats and steamers appeared, and the river was happy again.

"I may not be clean and pretty any more," sighed the river, "but I can see that I am now very useful."

105

On went the river until it reached the docks. Here it began to get excited because of all the great ships. Everyone seemed to be very busy, and all was hustle and bustle. It was a grand sight to see so many cargo ships and liners. All kinds of food were being unloaded from the large cargo ships ; food which had come from far-away lands across the sea. The liners, which took people by sea from one country to another, were even bigger and more beautiful. No wonder the river was excited.

" I shall never be able to carry such huge ships ! " cried the river. " I am not strong enough ! "

Then a wonderful thing happened. Suddenly the river met the sea and flowed into it.

"Now I can do it!" shouted the river with joy. "This is where I belong! This is why I could never stop! Now I am perfectly happy!"

*(Adapted)*

## DO YOU REMEMBER ?

1. What is the title of the story ?
2. What sound did the spring make ?
3. What did it become as it ran down the hill-side ?
4. What did the little girl do as it passed ?
5. What name is given to the other streams which joined it ?
6. Describe the first bridge across the stream.
7. What did the little boy say ?
8. What was the stream called when it became much bigger ?
9. What did the river do where the banks were not wide enough ?
10. Why was the river proud when it entered a small town ?
11. Why was the river sad when it entered a city ?
12. Why did the river become excited at the docks ?
13. What were the men doing on the cargo ships ?
14. What wonderful thing happened to the river ?
15. What did it say ?

LINER

SAILING SHIP

FISHING BOAT

TANKER

LIFEBOAT

CARGO SHIP

SUBMARINE

AIRCRAFT CARRIER

## CAN YOU TELL ?

1. The spring said, " Plop, plop, plop ! "

   Look at these words :—" Tick-tock ! " " Crack ! Crack ! " " Pitter-patter ! " " Pop ! " " Rat-tat-tat ! " " Toot ! Toot ! "

   Now put them in their sentences.
   (a) The cork gave a loud ............
   (b) ............ went the clock.
   (c) The motor-car sounded a warning ............
   (d) ............ went the rain on the window.
   (e) He knocked on the door with a sharp ...........
   (f) ............ went the lion-tamer's whip.

2. Put these in order (smallest first) :—

   (a) tea-pot, pail, kettle, cup.
   (b) city, village, country, town.
   (c) river, stream, spring, sea.

3. Do you know the name given to :—

   (a) the beginning of a river ?
   (b) the sides of a river ?
   (c) the end of a river ?
   (d) the streams which join it ?
   (e) where the water lies ?

4. Describe as many different kinds of bridges as you can.

5. Why does a river (a) get bigger and bigger ? (b) always keep moving ?

6. What name is given to :—(*a*) pipes which take away dirty water ? (*b*) big buildings where things are made ? (*c*) a place where many ships can load and unload cargoes ?

7. Name as many different kinds of boats or ships as you can.

8. Give the opposites of these words :—down, long, slowly, sad, dirty, wide, beautiful, whispered, laughed, entered.

---

### SOME THINGS TO DO

Draw and paint a picture of a yacht.

Tell your group about a trip in a boat.

Make a model of a boat or ship.

# 17

## RUMPEL-STILTS-KIN

ONCE upon a time, there lived a miller who had a beautiful daughter. He was always boasting about her, and he told every one how clever and lovely she was.

One day the king was out hunting, and he happened to call at the mill on his way home. As usual, the miller began to talk about his lovely daughter. He even boasted that she could spin straw into gold.

The king was delighted to hear such wonderful news. " Bring your daughter to the palace to-morrow ! " he said. " I will see if what you say is true ! "

Next day, the girl was brought before the king. At once he took her to a large room, which was full of straw.

" I want all this straw to be changed into gold by to-morrow morning ! " he ordered. Then he walked out, shut the door, and left her alone in the room.

The poor girl did not know what to do. At last she sat down and began to cry.

Suddenly the door opened, and in walked a strange little man. He was wearing a green suit, a green hat with a feather in it, and the funniest shoes you ever saw. They were long and narrow and had toes which were twisted like corkscrews.

" Good day ! " he said " Why are you crying ? "

"Oh!" replied the girl. "The king has ordered me to spin all this straw into gold, and I do not know how to do it."

"Will you give me your pretty necklace if I do it for you?" he asked.

"Certainly!" replied the girl, and she gave him her necklace.

The strange little man sat down at the spinning wheel and began to spin. Whir! Whir! Whir! The straw began to turn to gold. Whir! Whir! Whir! More gold and more gold. While he worked he sang this little song.

" Round about, round about,
Lo and behold !
Reel away, reel away,
Straw into gold ! "

Soon the room was full of gold, and the girl was very happy. When the strange little man was finished, he rose from his seat and slipped quietly out of the room.

Early next morning, the king came to see her. He was very surprised, when he saw the room full of gold. He was a very greedy king. He wanted her to make more gold, so that he would be very rich.

The king took her to another room which was full of straw. He asked her to change all the straw into gold. When he left the room, the poor girl sat down and cried.

Suddenly the door opened, and who should walk

115

in but the strange little man. " Why do you cry ? " he asked. " Did I not change the straw into gold for you ? "

" Yes," replied the girl, " but the king wants more straw changed into gold."

" Will you give me that pretty ring on your finger if I do it for you ? " he asked.

" Certainly ! " replied the girl, and she gave him her ring.

Again the strange little man sat down and began to spin. Again the straw was changed into gold.

When the king came to see her next morning, he was pleased to find another store of gold.

He took her to a much bigger room which was full of straw and said, " Spin all this straw into gold and you shall be my queen." When he left the room, the poor girl sat down and cried.

A few minutes later, the strange little man entered and said, " Why do you cry ? Twice I have changed all the straw into gold for you."

" Yes," replied the girl, " but the king wants more straw changed into gold. This is to be the last time, and if I do it, I shall be queen."

" If you become queen, will you give me your first child ? " he asked.

The poor girl stared at him in surprise. What a strange thing to ask !

At first she could not make up her mind, but at last she said, " Yes. I will give you my first child."

Once again the strange little man sat down to spin, and once again, the straw was changed into gold.

When the king came next morning, he was delighted to find another great store of gold.

Not long afterwards, they were married and she became queen. A few years later, a child was born and everybody was very happy. The queen had forgotten the strange little man, and her promise to him.

Then one day, as the young queen watched her baby in the cot, the door opened, and in walked the strange little man.

" I have come for your child," he said. " You must now keep your promise."

" No, no, no ! " replied the queen. " You can have all the riches in the kingdom, but do not take away my baby ! "

" Keep your promise ! " cried the little man.
" Give me the child ! "

The queen sat down and began to cry. She
begged him not to take the baby from her.

At last the little man said, " Very well ! I'll
tell you what I'll do. If you can find out my name
in three days, I will not take your child."

The poor queen spent the whole night thinking
of all the names she had ever heard. When the
little man came back next day, she was ready with
a big list of names.

119

" Is your name John ? " she asked. " No ! "
he replied. " James ? "  " No ! "  " Robert ? "
" No ! "  " William ? "  " No ! "  " George ? "
" No ! "  " Thomas ? "  " No ! "  " Richard ? "
" No ! "  " Peter ? "  " No ! "  " David ? "
" No ! "  " Joseph ? "  " No ! "

The queen gave many more names, but to every
name the strange little man said " No ! "

The next day, servants were sent out over all
the kingdom for more names, but still they could
not find it.

On the third and last day, one of her servants came to her and said, " High in the mountains, I came across a lonely little house. There I saw a strange little man, all dressed in green and wearing long shoes with curly toes. He was dancing round his little house and singing this song :—

" Merrily the feast I'll make,
To-day I'll brew, to-morrow bake ;
Merrily I'll dance and sing,
For next day will a stranger bring ;
Little does my lady dream,
That Rumpel-stilts-kin is my name ! "

The queen jumped with joy. She was sure that it was the same strange little man who came to see her.

When the strange little man arrived, she asked, "Is your name Short Legs?" "No!" "Big Ears?" "No!" "Long Nose?" "No!" "Are you Rumpel-stilts-kin?"

When he heard his name, the strange little man stamped his feet with rage. "You have cheated me!" he cried. "A witch must have told you! A witch must have told you!"

Suddenly, he dashed to the door, and ran out of the palace. No one ever saw him again. The queen was delighted, and said, "Thank goodness, we found out his name! The strange little man will never come back again, and my baby will not be taken away from me." *Grimm* (*Adapted*)

## DO YOU REMEMBER ?

1. What was the title of the story ?
2. Who was always boasting about his daughter ?
3. Who wanted the girl to be brought to the palace ?
4. What did the king ask her to do ?
5. Why did she sit down and cry ?
6. Who changed the straw into gold for her ?
7. What song did he sing as he worked ?
8. How often did the strange little man change straw into gold ?
9. What did she give him the first time ?
10. What did she give him the second time ?
11. What did he ask her to give him the third time ?
12. What had she to do to keep her child ?
13. What did the queen do to find out his name ?
14. What did a servant see at the lonely house in the mountains ?
15. What happened when the queen told him his name ?

123

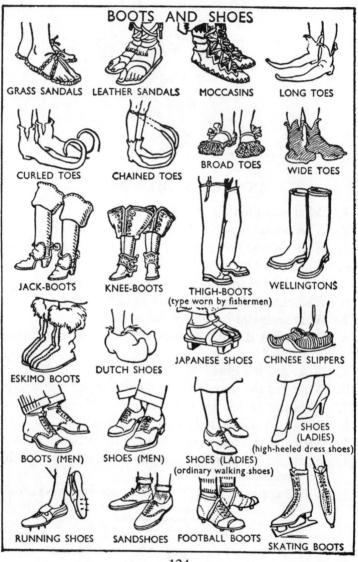

BOOTS AND SHOES

GRASS SANDALS     LEATHER SANDALS     MOCCASINS     LONG TOES

CURLED TOES     CHAINED TOES     BROAD TOES     WIDE TOES

JACK-BOOTS     KNEE-BOOTS     THIGH-BOOTS     WELLINGTONS
(type worn by fishermen)

ESKIMO BOOTS     DUTCH SHOES     JAPANESE SHOES     CHINESE SLIPPERS

BOOTS (MEN)     SHOES (MEN)     SHOES (LADIES)     SHOES (LADIES)
(ordinary walking shoes)     (high-heeled dress shoes)

RUNNING SHOES     SANDSHOES     FOOTBALL BOOTS     SKATING BOOTS

## CAN YOU TELL ?

1. Whir ! Whir ! Whir ! went the **spinning-wheel.**
Choo-choo-choo-choo ! went the...............
Bang ! went the...............
Ting-a-ling ! went the...............
Crash ! went the...............

2.
| One | More than one |
|-----|---------------|
| box | ............... |
| knife | ............... |
| child | ............... |
| roof | ............... |
| baby | ............... |

3. Put these words in their right places.
cup, bag, bottle, cake, bunch.
(a) a ............ of flowers,    (b) a ............ of tea,
(c) a ............ of sweets,    (d) a ............ of milk,
(e) a ............ of soap.

4. In the word **" lamb "** you do not sound the letter
" b."
What are the silent letters in :—hour, knee, talk,
wrong, knife, honest, calm, comb ?

5. Give one word instead of the two words underlined.
(a) The man was **not in.**
(b) The bag was **not heavy.**
(c) The pencil was **not sharp.**
(d) The river was **not deep.**
(e) The boy was **not polite.**

6. What did the girl have (*a*) round her neck ? (*b*) on her finger ?
   What do ladies sometimes have (*c*) in their ears ? (*d*) on their wrists ? (*e*) on their dresses ?

7. (*a*) Give three names of boys which begin with the letter **J**.
   (*b*) Give three names of girls which begin with the letter **A**.

8. What is the difference between :—
   (*a*) girls' shoes and boys' shoes, (*b*) sandals and slippers, (*c*) sandshoes and wellingtons ?

---

### SOME THINGS TO DO

Paint a colour picture of Rumpel-stilts-kin.

You have just found a flower made of gold. Write a story telling what you will do with the flower.

Make a model of Rumpel-stilts-kin's cottage.

## GOODBYE !

" GOODBYE ! " says the swallow, " to-night I
      must go,

For insects are few, and the chilly winds blow ! "

" Good-bye ! " says the toad, as he crawls off
      alone,

" I've found a good sleeping-place under a stone."

" Good-bye ! " says the snake, " I am going to
      creep

In this old hollow tree—I shall soon be asleep ! "

" Good-bye ! " says the hedgehog, " you'll see me
      no more,

In the ditch I shall doze—and perhaps I shall
      snore ! "

" Good-bye ! " says the frog, " to the pond I shall
      leap

And tuck myself up in the mud for a sleep."

" Good-bye, all you creatures, sleep winter away,
And come back with joy on a sunny spring day ! "

*Enid Blyton.*

# A HOT LAND . . . INDIA

JOHN and Mary had been invited by their Uncle Bob to spend a holiday with him in India. After a long sea-voyage, they reached this strange hot land, where so many things are different to what we see here.

When they arrived, Uncle Bob took them by car to his home. He stayed in the country, and his house had many large fields round it. In these fields were rows and rows of bushes.

" Uncle ! What kind of plants are those ? " asked John, pointing towards one of the fields.

"Those are tea-bushes," replied Uncle Bob. "I am a tea-planter."

Just after breakfast next morning, Uncle Bob said to them, "I have to do some shopping in town. Get ready and come with me. I am sure you will enjoy the trip."

On their way to town, they passed many carts which were drawn by oxen. The sun was very hot as they sped along the dry dusty roads. They saw the people, all brown in colour, and John and Mary stared in surprise at their dress.

The men wore long, loose shirts and, instead of trousers, they had cloths tied round their bodies. On their heads they had turbans. A

turban is a long strip of cloth rolled tightly round the head.

" Look ! " cried Mary. " The women look just like butterflies. They wear such lovely bright dresses . . . blue, pink, green, red, yellow."

" Yes," replied Uncle Bob. " They do look beautiful. The dress is a long piece of cloth draped round the waist and over the shoulders. It is called a sari."

As they passed through a village, they saw many small houses. " Uncle ! Could we have a peep inside a real Indian house ? " asked John. " I cannot see any chimneys and the fireplaces are outside . . . against the walls."

Uncle Bob stopped the car, and spoke to a woman who stood in the doorway of a house. He talked to her in strange words, which they did not understand. She smiled, and Uncle Bob told them to go inside.

"See!" said their uncle. "The walls are made of clay bricks, and the floor is of hard dried mud. There isn't much here . . . a bamboo bed with grass woven in and out, a wooden plough for the fields, a large jug for water, and four big jars filled with fruit and rice."

They left the house and went back to the car. Soon they came to a place with many narrow streets. This was the town. They got out of the car, and walked along a narrow street towards the shops.

" What strange shops ! " said Mary. " They are wide open with no windows, and the shop-keepers are all sitting on the ground in front of them."

John was not listening. He was too busy looking at much stranger things. He laughed when he saw a barber shaving his customer by the side of the road. His eyes nearly popped out of his head when he saw a man playing on a pipe and a snake rising from a basket in front of him.

As he turned to speak to his uncle, he saw another strange sight. A cow came down the street, walked over to a shop, and began to eat some of the food which was on show.

" Uncle ! " cried John. " Look at that cow ! It is eating the food in the shop.

132

Why don't the shopkeepers drive it away ? "

" No, John. They won't chase it away," replied Uncle Bob. " There are many different races in India, and some of them believe that the cow is a sacred animal. Other creatures, such as the monkey, the cat, the eagle, and the bull are sacred too."

Suddenly a crowd of men in long white robes came down the street. They all looked tired and weary, as if they had walked far.

" Those men are pilgrims," said Uncle Bob. " They are going to bathe in the River Ganges. To the Indians, it is a holy river."

All too soon they had to return to the car. On the way back they heard the loud blowing of trumpets, and John and Mary looked at each other in wonder.

" By Jove ! " cried Uncle Bob. " Look yonder at the edge of the jungle ! A hunt is on ! See the men on the backs of the elephants ! They are hunting the most dreaded beast in India . . . the tiger."

" What a strange yet wonderful country ! " said John.

" Yes," replied Mary. " I will write to mother to-night. I must tell her all about India."

*(Adapted)*

## DO YOU REMEMBER ?

1. What is the title of the story ?
2. Who invited John and Mary to India ?
3. What was his work ?
4. What colour were the people ?
5. How were the men dressed ?
6. How were the women dressed ?
7. Describe a small village house.
8. What was strange about the shops ?
9. Why did John laugh at the barber ?
10. When did his eyes nearly pop out of his head ?
11. What was the cow doing ?
12. Why did they not chase it away ?
13. Where were the men in long white robes going ?
14. What did the loud blowing of trumpets mean ?
15. How did the Indians hunt the tiger ?

---

# BOYS' DRESS

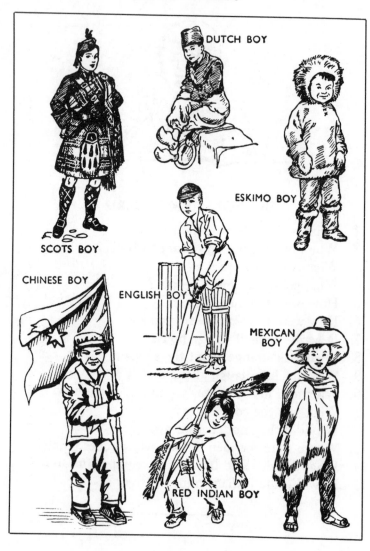

DUTCH BOY

ESKIMO BOY

SCOTS BOY

CHINESE BOY

ENGLISH BOY

MEXICAN BOY

RED INDIAN BOY

SPANISH GIRL

JAPANESE GIRL

RUSSIAN GIRL

INDIAN GIRL

BAVARIAN GIRL

BURMESE GIRL

AFRICAN GIRL

## CAN YOU TELL ?

1. The dresses were blue, pink, green, red, and yellow.
   Name as many other colours as you can.

2. The tiger is a fierce wild animal.
   Name other fierce wild animals.

3. An Indian is **brown** in colour.

   What colour is (1) an African negro, (2) a Red Indian, (3) a Chinese, (4) an Arab, (5) a German ?

4. The carts were drawn by **oxen.**
   Name other animals which are used to pull or carry loads.

5. On their heads, the Indians **wore a turban.**

   Describe these hats and draw them:—bowler, " tile," cowboy, sailor, Boy Scout, Boys' Brigade.

6. The people living in **India** are called **Indian** people.

   What are the people living in these countries called ? Ireland, England, Scotland, Wales, France, Germany, China, Spain, Greece, Holland.

7. How are these animals hunted ?
   Tigers, lions, rabbits, foxes, deer.

8. What would you wear:—

   (a) to play football, (b) to go swimming, (c) to travel in a cold land, (d) to travel in a hot land?

## PINOCCHIO THE PUPPET

IN days of long ago, people used to go to puppet shows as to-day they go to picture houses. The plays were acted by dressed-up wooden dolls, which were made to move by pulling wires.

One day, a man called Geppetto visited his friend Mr. Cherry, the joiner, and asked him for a piece of wood to make a puppet.

"I am not going to make a common puppet like Punch or Judy," said Geppetto. "This one will be a very clever puppet who will be able to dance and sing."

"Here is a fine hard piece of wood," replied Mr. Cherry. "I will take off the bark with my axe."

Just as he was about to strike it, he heard a little voice say, "Please do not hit me hard."

139

Mr. Cherry dropped the wood in astonishment. He looked at Geppetto and asked him if he had spoken. Geppetto shook his head to show that he hadn't. Mr. Cherry lifted the piece of wood and struck it a sharp blow with his axe.

" Oh ! You've hurt me ! You've hurt me ! " cried the same little voice sadly.

The joiner dropped the wood again, but this time it struck Geppetto on the leg and made him jump with pain. " You villain ! " cried Geppetto. " I did not think that you would strike an old friend." Then he picked up the piece of wood, and set off limping for home.

Geppetto lived in a little room at the top of a long flight of stairs. As soon as he arrived, he took up his tools and set to work. First he wedged the piece of wood firmly, so that it could not move. "You're hurting me!" cried a little voice.

Geppetto stared at the piece of wood in surprise. "You can speak, can you?" he said. "Just wait for an hour or two, and I'll make you into a little man."

He took his plane, and started to smooth the bit of wood. While he was running the plane up and down, he heard the same little voice say, "Stop it! You're tickling me!"

Geppetto next took a knife and began to carve the puppet's head, his hair, his ears, and his eyes. Then a very strange thing happened. As soon as he had carved the puppet's nose, it began to grow. It grew and grew and grew, until it was twice as long as his ears. Geppetto tried to cut it down, but it always grew to the same size again.

When the mouth was finished, the puppet began to laugh and make fun of him. " Stop laughing ! " cried Geppetto crossly. The puppet stopped laughing, but put out its tongue at him. Geppetto pretended not to notice, and kept on working until he had finished the chin, the neck, the shoulders, the body, the arms, and the hands.

Geppetto had just finished the hands, when his wig was snatched from his head. He turned round quickly, and saw his wig in the puppet's hand.

" Now, my little man ! " he cried. " Give me back my wig at once ! " Instead of handing it back, the puppet tried it on his own head, but it nearly smothered him.

" You bad rascal ! " shouted Geppetto. " You have started to disobey me already ! You must learn to do as you are told ! "

The puppet was sorry, and tried to put the wig back on his master's head. " That's better," said Geppetto. " Now, be a good little man."

When Geppetto had finished the feet, he took the puppet and placed him standing on the floor. At first the puppet's legs would not move, but Geppetto showed him how to walk.

" Now, see if you can do it by yourself," said Geppetto. Suddenly the puppet ran across the room. The door was open, and off he went down the stairs. He could not stop, and was soon out on the street.

" Stop him ! Stop him ! " shouted Geppetto as he ran after him. The people were astonished at the sight of a wooden puppet running on its own, and they stepped quickly out of its way.

144

Luckily, there was a policeman at the end of the street. The puppet tried to pass between his legs, but the policeman cleverly caught him by his long nose.

" Naughty little man, home you come ! " cried Geppetto, after he had thanked the policeman.

Back went the puppet and his master along the street. Many of the crowd, who had seen the strange race, filled Geppetto's hat with coppers because he had made such a clever puppet.

*Pinocchio—The Story of a Puppet*

## DO YOU REMEMBER ?

1. What was the title of the story ?
2. What was the name of the joiner ?
3. Who asked him for a bit of wood ?
4. Why did he want the piece of wood ?
5. What happened when Mr. Cherry struck the wood with the axe ?
6. Why did Geppetto become very angry ?
7. Where did Geppetto live ?
8. What happened when he started to smooth the piece of wood ?
9. What did Geppetto use to carve the puppet ?
10. What was strange about the puppet's nose ?
11. What happened when Geppetto finished the hands ?
12. What happened when he finished the feet ?
13. Where did the puppet go ?
14. Who caught him ?
15. Why did the people put coppers in Geppetto's hat ?

> **Dressmaker, engineer, gardener hairdresser,**
> **joiner, shoemaker.**

(a) Which of the above people use, at their work, the tools shown below?

(b) Here is a much harder question.
Can you name each tool?

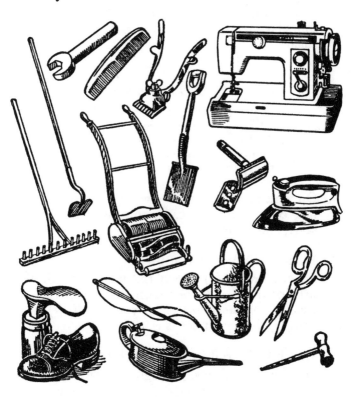

## CAN YOU TELL ?

1. Point to these parts of the body :—hair, eyes, ears, nose, cheeks, mouth, chin, neck, shoulders, arms, elbows, wrists, hands, fingers, back, chest, waist, legs, knees, ankles, feet, toes.

2. Which of these words should always start with a **Capital Letter** ?

   table, james, chair, mary, garden, basket, ladder, thursday, feathers, forest, barrel, july, floor, france, sugar.

3. 

   | *One* | *More than one* |
   |-------|-----------------|
   | shelf | ............... |
   | lady | ............... |
   | goose | ............... |
   | penny | ............... |
   | sheep | ............... |

4. On which parts of the body are these worn ?
   hat, collar, gloves, beads, ring, wig, bangle, ribbon, scarf, shoes, belt.

5. What would you use to :—
   (*a*) cut bread, (*b*) sweep the floor, (*c*), stir the fire, (*d*) dry the dishes, (*e*) polish the table, (*f*) stir the tea, (*g*) eat meat, (*h*) clean your teeth, (*i*) tidy your hair, (*j*) darn your socks ?

6. Which is the right word in each sentence ?
   (*a*) The boy (threw, through) a stone.
   (*b*) Mother uses (flower, flour) for baking.

(c) The girl bought (to, too, two) books.

(d) The farmer has to (sow, so, sew) the seed in spring.

(e) The sailor (rode, rowed, road) the boat across the river.

7. 

### What ?

(1) The cow gives us.............. (2) Windows are made of.............,

### When ?

(3) We can see the stars.............. (4) We go to church..............

### Where ?

(5) We saw four little eggs.............. (6) The bees lived..............

### How ?

(7) He dug the garden.............. (8) She sharpened her pencil..............

8. Describe a Punch and Judy show.

---

### SOME THINGS TO DO

Draw a puppet man and woman each with a big nose. Give them names.

Imagine you are walking past a fruit tree and it speaks to you. Write a story about this.

Make a model puppet.

# THE MICE

THE merry mice stay in their holes,
　　And hide themselves by day;
But, when the house is still at night,
The rogues come out to play.

They climb upon the pantry shelf,
And taste of all they please;
They drink the milk that's set for cream,
And nibble bread and cheese.

But if they chance to hear the cat,
Their feast will soon be done;
They'll scamper off to hide themselves,
As fast as they can run.

Some tiny mice live in the fields,
And feed on flies and corn;
And in a pretty hanging nest,
The little ones are born.

When winter comes they burrow holes,
And line them soft with hay;
And while the snow is on the ground,
They sleep the time away.

*Anonymous.*

## AN UNSEEN FOE

ONE day a shepherd, who lived in a far-away land, went out to gather honey. After he had searched for quite a long time, he spied a big hollow tree-trunk.

Round the top of the tree, he heard the buzz of many bees. In order to protect himself, he pulled a net over his head and neck, and put on a pair of gloves. He climbed to the top to look inside. When he peeped down, he saw to his delight, a large honeycomb.

The shepherd bent over, and scooped out some honey into a tin, which was tied to his belt. As he stretched out to get more, he lost his balance, and tumbled into the hollow trunk. As he fell, he grabbed at the honeycomb, and pulled part of it with him.

When the shepherd reached the bottom, he was very frightened but not hurt. The angry bees attacked him, and buzzed loudly to and fro, but they could not harm him. He tried several times to climb up the inside of the tree, but he failed each time. He was shut inside the tree, and it seemed as if there was no way out.

Two whole days went by, and the shepherd was still in his strange prison. Whenever he heard a sound, he shouted with all his might, but no one heard him. He was not hungry, because he had plenty of honey to eat, but he was very, very thirsty.

152

On the morning of the third day, he heard a loud scratching outside the foot of the tree.

" My goodness ! " he said to himself. " It must be a bear on the look-out for honey. What on earth shall I do, if he comes in here ! "

Bears are very fond of honey, and are always on the prowl in search of it. They are not afraid of the bees, because their coats of fur are so thick that they are protected from the stings of the angry insects.

By the sound of the scratching on the bark, he knew that the creature was climbing the tree. When he looked up, he saw, to his horror, a huge brown bear. The animal was scrambling over the top and coming down upon him inside the trunk.

153

Suddenly the shepherd felt his courage come back to him. "Anything is better than to stay here and starve to death. I will give Mr. Bruin the shock of his life."

The bear was coming down backwards and did not see the shepherd. As soon as the animal's tail was within his reach, he caught it in his strong hands. Suddenly he gave it a quick hard pull.

The bear gave a loud howl of pain and surprise. Without turning to see what had hurt him, the frightened creature began to scramble up out of the trunk as quickly as he could.

At that very moment, a clever idea came into

the shepherd's head. As the huge animal clawed his way up the inside of the tree, the man flung his arms round the bear's hind legs.

This made the bear more frightened than ever. The animal struggled desperately to get to the top of the trunk and escape from his attacker. The bold shepherd held on to the animal, until at last they reached the open air.

As soon as he was safe at the top, the shepherd let go his hold on the bear. The bear, now free from his terrible foe, slid quickly down the outside of the trunk and hurried off into the forest.

When he could no longer hear the grunts of the frightened animal, the joyful shepherd climbed down the tree and set off for home. His wife and family were delighted to see him. They thought something dreadful had happened to him.

After he had eaten some food, he told them of his strange adventure. They all laughed and joked about the way in which he had escaped.

The biggest laugh of all rang through the little cottage when the youngest of his children said, " Father ! The bear must have thought that you were the bogey-man ! "

*(Adapted)*

## DO YOU REMEMBER ?

1. What is the title of the story ?
2. For what was the shepherd searching ?
3. What sound came from the top of the hollow trunk ?
4. How did he protect himself ?
5. What did the shepherd take from the honeycomb ?
6. Where did he put the honey ?
7. How did he fall down into the hollow trunk ?
8. Why was he afraid ?
9. When did he hear the bear ?
10. What did the animal do ?
11. Why did the bear not see the shepherd ?
12. How did the shepherd frighten the bear ?
13. How did the shepherd escape ?
14. To whom did he tell his strange story ?
15. What did his youngest child say ?

# DEFENCE AND ATTACK

WALRUS
TUSKS

GOAT
HORNS

ELEPHANT
TUSKS

TIGER
CLAWS

CROCODILE
TEETH/TAIL

BEE
STING

SNAKE
FANGS

PORCUPINE
SPINES

EAGLE
BEAK/TALONS

CRAB
NIPPERS

OSTRICH
FEET

TURTLE
SHELL

BOA CONSTRICTOR
CRUSHING

## CAN YOU TELL ?

1. **Bears** are very fond of **honey.**

   Which animals are very fond of:—bones, milk, cheese, nuts, carrots, fish, lettuce, grass ?

2. **Honey** is found in a **comb.**

   What is usually found in a:—kettle, purse, jar, caddy, envelope ?

3. The shepherd called the bear **" Bruin."**

   Which animals are called:—Jumbo, Bunny, Neddy, Jacko, Dobbin, Fido, Reynard, Leo ?

4. The bear in the story was a **brown** bear.

   (*a*) What is a **white** bear called ?
   (*b*) Name other animals which are usually brown in colour.

5. **Honey** has a very **sweet taste.**

   Which of the following are very sweet:—bread, sugar, jam, butter, cheese, cakes, milk, syrup ?

6. The bear is **protected** from the stings of bees by his **thick fur coat.**

   How do these creatures save themselves from harm:— Snail, hedgehog, rabbit, mouse, monkey, cow, horse, elephant ?

7. The bear **climbed** up the tree.

   Name any other animals which can climb trees.

8. Give the **opposites** of these words in the story:— cold, far, long, top, large, quick, inside, thick, lost, clever, youngest, pulled.

# ALI BABA AND
# THE FORTY THIEVES

LONG ago in the land of Persia, there lived a poor wood-cutter called Ali Baba. One day, while he was working in the forest, he saw some horsemen coming his way. They were shouting and making a loud noise, and poor Ali Baba knew at once that they were a band of robbers. As quickly as he could, he climbed up the nearest tree, and hid among the branches.

As they passed close to the tree, Ali Baba counted forty men in all. Suddenly they stopped, and got off their horses. The captain of the band walked forward, and struck the face of a great rock with his hand. At the same time he cried in a loud voice, " Open Sesame." Strange to say, a door in the rock opened, and the men entered what seemed to be a large cave.

160

Ali Baba nearly fell off the tree in surprise. This must be the place where the robbers hid their treasure. He watched and waited until they came out. He saw that each man looked very happy and was carrying a heavy bundle.

When they had all gone, Ali Baba climbed down the tree and went to the rock. He struck it with his hand and cried, " Open Sesame." The door in the rock opened, and he went forward to peep inside.

161

His eyes and mouth opened wide at what he saw. There were bags of gold, and silver, and heaps of jewels piled on the floor. Ali Baba entered the cave and carried some of the sacks outside. Then he said to himself, " How can I take home such a heavy load ? "

Suddenly he remembered his faithful donkey. He had left it tied to a tree while he was cutting and gathering wood in the forest. Ali Baba rushed to where the animal was, and emptied the baskets of wood. He then led the donkey to the cave.

Ali Baba put the sacks of treasure into the baskets, and carefully shut the door of the cave. He hurried home, and hid the bags in a corner of the stable, so that no one would know about his lucky discovery.

The wood-cutter visited the cave several times, and always returned with a load of riches. He told his wife and son about the treasure in the cave, and they were delighted at his good fortune. At once they made grand plans as to what they would do with their money.

163

So, from being a poor wood-cutter, Ali Baba became the richest man in that part of the country. He built a fine palace, and had many servants. The people wondered how he had become rich so quickly.

After a time, the robbers returned to their cave. "Someone has been here," cried the chief. "See! Some thief knows our secret and has stolen most of our treasure. We must find him at once and kill him."

The robbers hurried away and spied in all the nearby villages. They found out that Ali Baba had suddenly become very rich, and no one knew how he had got the money.

" Ali Baba must be the thief ! " cried the captain of the band of robbers. " Now we must plan to kill him." Suddenly he said with a wicked smile, " I know how we can do it. You will go to the villages round about, and bring me forty mules and forty large jars. Fill one of the jars with oil, but all the others must be left empty."

When this was done, the captain led the way to the fine new palace of Ali Baba. He told Ali Baba that he was a merchant, and wished food and shelter for the night. Ali Baba made him welcome, and told him to store the jars in the cellar.

When the jars had been placed in the cellar, each robber climbed into a jar and hid there. They were to wait in the jars until they got a signal from their master.

165

Ali Baba was very kind to the captain, and gave him a fine supper in the lovely dining-room. While they were eating, Morgiana the maidservant, noticed that the lamps needed more oil. She went down to the cellar to fetch some.

She lifted the lid of the first jar. " Is it time ? " asked the robber inside. " No ! Not yet ! " replied Morgiana in surprise. Then she said to herself, " This must be a wicked plot to harm my master."

She raised the lid of the second jar very carefully. This happened to be the one which was full of oil. She filled her jug with oil from the jar, and went quickly to the kitchen. There she heated the oil until it was boiling.

Morgiana carefully lifted the jug of boiling oil, and tip-toed back to the cellar. So quietly did she return, that not one of the robbers heard her. Quickly she ran round all the jars, and poured some boiling oil into each of them.

What a dreadful noise there was ! All the robbers were howling in pain and shouting for mercy. Ali Baba's servants rushed to the cellar to find out what was wrong. When they saw the robbers, they at once attacked and captured them. Some of the servants ran back upstairs, and captured the robber chief before he could escape. A few minutes later, the robbers were taken away to prison.

Ali Baba was very pleased to see the last of the forty thieves. He thanked Morgiana for the clever way in which she had saved his life. Not long afterwards she married his son, and Ali Baba gave them a large part of the treasure as a wedding gift.

(*Adapted*)

## DO YOU REMEMBER ?

1. What is the title of the story ?
2. Where did the story take place ?
3. Why did Ali Baba work in the forest ?
4. What did he do when he saw the robbers ?
5. How did the robber chief enter the cave ?
6. What was in the cave ?
7. Where did Ali Baba hide the treasure ?
8. How did he show that he had become very rich ?
9. How did the robbers get into the palace ?
10. Why did Morgiana go to the cellar ?
11. What happened when she went to the first jar ?
12. What did she take from the second jar ?
13. Why did she go to the kitchen ?
14. How did Morgiana defeat the robbers ?
15. How did Ali Baba reward her ?

MODERN HOUSE

KITCHEN

BEDROOM

DINING ROOM

SITTING ROOM

## CAN YOU TELL?

1. Show how you:—tip-toe, march, limp, shuffle, stamp.

2. Each of these is done with your **eyes** or **ears** or **voice**. Which? Speak, see, look, whisper, talk, hear, peep, stare, listen, shout, sing, spy.

3. We say " A band of **robbers.**"

   Complete the following:—
   (1) an army of ................, (2) a gang of ................,
   (3) a team of ................, (4) a crew of ................,
   (5) a choir of ................

4. **In the story,** the oil in the cellar was kept in ..........
   and the gold and silver in the cave was stored in ............

   In what would you expect to find:—(1) money, (2) jam, (3) milk, (4) sugar, (5) bread, (6) sauce, (7) coal, (8) tea?

5. Which of these men work with **wood**?

   barber, wood-cutter, joiner, cobbler, baker, carpenter, lumberjack, miner, tailor, timber merchant.

6. In which **room** of a house is it usual to:—

   (1) eat, (2) sleep, (3) wash your face, (4) cook food, (5) hang your coat, (6) play the piano?

7. Page number **one** is the **first** page.

   What do we say for pages two, three, four, five, six?

8. At the time of the story, **oil lamps** were used to give light. In what other ways can we get light?

---

## THE SHEPHERD

I KNOW a man who's old and wise,
  He reads the wind, he reads the skies,
He knows when storms will blow his way,
He knows what rain will fall each day.

He'll take you where the primrose shines,
He knows the early celandines,
He names each bird that by him flies,
His eyes are very blue and wise.

All day and night he tends the sheep,
He hears them bleating in his sleep,
There's not a lamb upon the farm,
He hasn't carried in his arm.

I wish I knew the things he knows,
The night-time skies, the wind that blows,
The singing birds, the bleating cries—
I wish I were a shepherd wise.

*Enid Blyton.*

## THE WONDERFUL ANT

"TOM! Come here quickly!" cried Mary. "Look at this tiny insect crawling across the grass! It is carrying a crumb of bread which is bigger than itself!"

"It's an ant," replied her brother, as he came over to watch. "I expect he is taking it home for tea."

"He is very strong for his size," said Mary.

"Oh yes!" replied Tom. "An ant can lift and carry loads which are much heavier than himself. I remember a funny thing that happened last summer."

"You know Fred Smith's little dog Spotty? He was barking and running after rabbits. Suddenly he stopped and began to dig up what he thought was a rabbit's burrow. It turned out to be an ant-hill instead."

" Spotty got a fright when he found ants crawling all over his head and nose. Some of the poor ants were frightened too, and they ran about here and there with the baby ants in their mouths."

" Silly," replied his sister. " Do you expect me to believe that ? "

" It's true ! " cried Tom. " I saw it with my own eyes ! "

" I believe you," said a voice behind them. They looked round and saw Uncle Jim.

" Ants are wonderful creatures," said Uncle Jim. " They are a lesson to us in many ways. They are clean and tidy, always busy and never idle. Each ant does his own kind of work for the good of the whole family."

" Tell us all about them," said Tom.

Uncle Jim stopped to light his pipe and then began, " The mother ant lays her eggs in a little hole she has burrowed in the ground. From the eggs are hatched tiny white grubs which have no legs. They must be fed just like children."

" These little grubs grow and grow and spin coats or cocoons round themselves. When the coats are finished they stop eating and seem to go to sleep."

" Are they sleeping ? " asked Mary.

" No," replied Uncle Jim. " For three months they stay inside their coats, but all this time they are changing into ants. Then at last the great day comes. Slowly out of the coats come little insects.

" Their bodies are in two parts joined by a narrow waist. They have six legs and two long ' feelers ' which grow out from their heads. With these ' feelers ' they can hear and smell and touch."

Tom and Mary smiled, and their uncle went on :

" When the young ants grow up, they must help about the home. As Mother Ant is still laying eggs she needs some of them to take care of the grubs, and to look after their little brothers and sisters. These are the nurse ants."

" What about the others ? " asked Tom.

" The others help in different ways," said Uncle Jim. " They all work hard. Some make the home bigger, and dig out little passages like the streets of a town. Some keep the home clean and tidy, and carry away any rubbish."

" Some go out to bring in food, and even make a store for the winter. Some are like soldiers, and are always ready to defend their home against any foes."

" The strangest kind of all are those which keep ' pets.' These pets are insects called greenfly, and they give up a sweet, sticky kind of honey, when stroked gently. They are very useful to the ants, who feed them, and look after them well."

There was silence for a moment and then Mary said, " Isn't that wonderful ? "

" Yes," replied Tom. " But all the same, I'm glad I'm not an ant. Fancy having hundreds of little brothers and sisters to take out for walks every day."

## DO YOU REMEMBER ?

1. What was the title of the story ?
2. What was (*a*) the boy's name ? (*b*) the girl's name ?
3. Which tiny insect crawled across the grass ?
4. What was it carrying ?
5. What was the little dog's name ?
6. What mistake did Spotty make ?
7. Who told Tom and Mary all about ants ?
8. In what ways can ants be a lesson to us ?
9. Who lays the eggs ?
10. What comes out of the eggs ?
11. How do the grubs live ?
12. How long do they stay inside their cocoons ?
13. Describe an ant.
14. Tell the different ways in which ants help in the home.
15. Why would Tom not like to be an ant ?

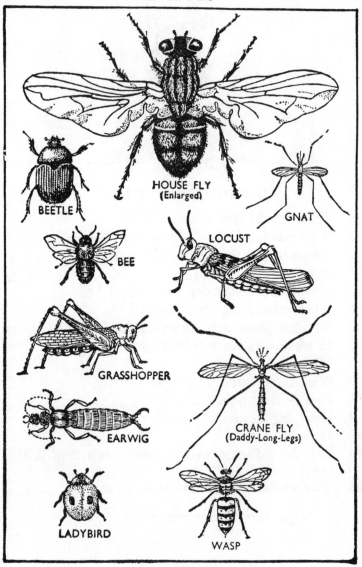

HOUSE FLY
(Enlarged)

BEETLE

GNAT

BEE

LOCUST

GRASSHOPPER

EARWIG

CRANE FLY
(Daddy-Long-Legs)

LADYBIRD

WASP

## CAN YOU TELL ?

1. The ant uses its **" feelers "** to **hear**, to **smell**, and to **touch.** What do we use to (*a*) hear, (*b*) smell, (*c*) touch ?

2. These words show **size.** Put a suitable word after each.

   (*a*) A tiny ............, (*b*) A big ............, (*c*) A little ............, (*d*) A large ............, (*e*) A small ............, (*f*) A great ............, (*g*) A wee ............, (*h*) A huge ............

3. Ants use their **mouths** to carry the young ones to safety. Do you know of any other creatures which do the same with their babies ?

4. Ants help the home in different ways. How do these ants help ?—nurses, soldiers, cleaners, food-hunters, builders, pet-keepers.

5. The **ant** is a busy, **hard worker.**
   Can you name any other creatures which are hard workers ?

6. An **ant** has **six legs.** How many legs has a :—hen, elephant, bee, rabbit, goose, beetle, camel, fly, monkey, tiger, gorilla, wasp ?

7. (*a*) Name three insects which can fly.
   (*b*) Name three insects which crawl but cannot fly.

8. We say "**a crumb of bread.**" Complete the following :—

(a) a piece of ............ (b) a spoonful of ............

(c) a drop of ............ (d) a scrap of ................

(e) a speck of............ (f) a puff of ................

(g) a pinch of............ (h) a blade of................

(i) a splinter of......... (j) a ray of....................

---

### SOME THINGS TO DO

Draw an ant hill to show some of the passages inside.

Your spaceship lands on a planet where the natives are all large ants. Write of your adventures.

Make a large model of an ant.

# 26

# THE WOODEN HORSE OF TROY

MANY, many years ago, the people of Greece and the people of Troy were at war with each other. The Greeks were so angry that they set off in their ships to attack Troy. They wanted to capture the city and burn it to the ground.

When the Greeks reached Troy, they found that it was not going to be easy to destroy it. There was a great high wall all round the city, and the gates were closed and defended by many brave men.

For ten long years, the Greeks tried hard to beat the Trojans. Time and again they attacked the gates and tried to climb the walls, but they were always driven back. Many heroes on both sides died in the fighting which took place.

At last one of the Greek leaders thought of a

very clever plan. He knew that Troy could only be captured if some of his soldiers could manage to get inside the city.

This leader told his men to build a great wooden horse. The horse was to be hollow, and big enough to hold some soldiers inside it. The men set to work with a will, and before long, the great horse was finished.

When all was ready, some of the Greek soldiers climbed inside it and shut the door. It was so

182

well made that no one would know that there was a door. The Greeks then pulled and pushed the wooden horse up to one of the gates and left it there.

When this was done, the Greek army went to their ships and sailed away. They left one man behind, and he hid himself in a wood. For the first time in ten years, no Greek soldiers were to be seen near the city.

The people of Troy could not believe their eyes when they saw the Greek ships sail away. They jumped and danced for joy. The Trojans thought that their foes had given up the fight and were

going home. Little did they know that this was a part of the Greek plan. The ships sailed away from Troy but, as soon as they were out of sight, they stopped and waited.

The Trojans saw the great wooden horse in front of one of the gates, and they wondered why the Greeks had left it there. Soon after, they opened the gate, and ran out to look at it more closely.

" What a wonderful horse ! " they cried. " Look how big it is ! Why did the Greeks leave it here ? "

Suddenly there was a shout. Someone had seen and caught the man, who had been left behind.

" A Greek ! " cried the people. " He must be a spy ! Kill him ! "

" Do not harm him ! " shouted the Trojan leader. " Bring him to me at once ! Perhaps he can tell us about the wooden horse."

The poor man was brought before him. " You are a Greek spy and you deserve to die," said the Trojan leader. " However, we shall spare your life, if you tell us why this great wooden horse was left here."

" That is an easy question to answer," replied the Greek. " The horse was made as a gift to the gods. The gods will protect whoever owns it."

" If that is so, why did the Greeks not take it away with them ? " asked the Trojan leader.

" It was far too big," said the Greek. " It could not be carried away on a ship."

" Good ! " cried the Trojan. " We will take it into Troy, and the gods will now be on our side."

The great wooden horse was dragged into the city. Once it was inside the gate, the Trojans

began to feast and make merry. The Greeks had gone home, and everybody was happy. There was no need to defend the gates, or keep watch from the walls.

Late that night, when the people of Troy were fast asleep, strange things began to happen.

The Greek soldiers, who were inside the horse, quietly opened the door and climbed down ropes to the ground. It was dark and no one saw them. One soldier went down to the shore and lit a signal fire. The others opened all the city gates. Quickly the Greek ships returned to Troy, and the soldiers rushed into the city through the open gates.

The people of Troy were taken by surprise. They woke to find the Greek soldiers setting fire to their houses. The Trojans fought bravely, but soon the whole city was in flames. When Troy had been burnt to the ground, the Greeks sailed away once more. They had won victory by a clever trick and the long war was ended.

(*Adapted*)

187

## DO YOU REMEMBER ?

1. What is the title of the story ?
2. Who were at war with each other ?
3. How did the Greeks reach Troy ?
4. What was round the city ?
5. How long did the Greeks try to beat the Trojans ?
6. Who thought of a very clever plan ?
7. What did he tell his men to do ?
8. Why was the horse made hollow and so big ?
9. Where did they put it ?
10. What did the Greek army do ?
11. Why did the Trojans jump and dance for joy ?
12. Why did they wonder at the great wooden horse ?
13. Who told them why it was made ?
14. What did the Trojans do with the horse ?
15. Tell what happened late that night.

188

WALLED CITY

BATTERING RAM

BALLISTA

TORTOISE

ARCHER

SPEARMAN

SWORDSMAN

# 27

# ANANSI AND THE FAIRIES

ANANSI, the spider, made up his mind to go to Port of Spain. When night fell he lay down to sleep in a wood and there the fairies found him. With their hands joined they danced round him in a ring singing:

"You have the power to change your shape to anything you choose. If you keep the King's command one day you shall see Fairyland. You have only to wish".

When Anansi awoke he felt hungry and sighed "I wish I had something to eat". At once a dish of roast goat was put before him. Then he wished for paw paw and it came in the same way. Feeling a little tired he wished to be a donkey. As soon as he had wished, he became a donkey. Next he wished to be a bird then a dog and last of all a horse. He galloped along the road scaring the people who were walking there by suddenly changing from a horse into a bird. Flying down towards them he would suddenly change into a crocodile. That sent them running back to their village.

He felt tired again because it was late afternoon and so fell asleep once more. The next morning, after a good breakfast of chocolate and cake and ice cream and lemonade Anansi decided he would have some fun.

A man walked down the road. He was trying to find his donkey which had wandered into a wood. Anansi at once changed himself into a donkey. When the man caught and mounted him Anansi set off for a muddy stream which was beside the road. As soon as he reached the stream he turned himself into a bird leaving the poor man to fall into the water.

191

Seeing Port of Spain in the distance he made up his mind to be a window cleaner. "Window cleaner" he called as he walked along the street carrying a bucket, cloth and ladder. Up came a woman from a big house asking him to clean her windows but Anansi changed into a bird and as he flew away he poured the water from the bucket all over her.

He next became a poor beggar sitting by the roadside. When an old lady was going to give him some money he changed into a little boy and skipped off laughing "Ho, ho, ho".

The King, who had given Anansi his wonderful power, decided that he must not play any more pranks. That night as he slept the King said "Anansi, you will come with me to Fairyland tonight". Anansi went off to Fairyland with the King and was never seen in Trinidad again.

Printed and bound in Great Britain by
Bell and Bain Ltd., Glasgow